MW00979018

SEASONS OF GRACE:
from Wilderness to Wonder

~ Victor Shepherd ~

Other books by Victor Shepherd:
So Great a Cloud of Witnesses
Ponder and Pray
Making Sense of Christian Faith
The Nature and Function of Faith in the Theology of John Calvin

© 1994 by Victor A. Shepherd

CONCEPT & EDITING: Lori Elizabeth Gwynne
COVER DESIGN: Davis & Associates
TEXT DESIGN/PRODUCTION: Wendelina O'Keefe
PRINTING: DFR Printing Ltd.

Published by Creative Bound Inc.
Box 424, Carp, Ontario K0A 1L0 (613) 831-3641

All rights reserved. No part of this publication may be reproduced,
stored in a retrieval system, or transmitted in any form or by any means,
electronic, mechanical, photocopying, recording, or otherwise, without the
prior written permission of the Publisher.

Printed in Canada

ISBN: 0-921165-36-6

CANADIAN CATALOGUING IN PUBLICATION DATA

Shepherd, Victor A.,   1944–
    Seasons of grace : from wilderness to wonder

ISBN 0-921165-36-6

    1. Spiritual life – – Christianity. I. Title.

BV4832.2.S44 1994   248   C94-90543-6

Dedication

*To my Streetsville United Church congregation
of sixteen years –
I remain "thankful for your partnership in the gospel
from the first day until now."
(Philippians 1:5)*

CONTENTS

Autumn
Hope in the Wilderness

The Wonder of God's Grace

Winter
Pain in the Wilderness

The Wonder of God's Word

Spring

Awakenings in the Wilderness

The Wonder of God's Love

Summer

Temptations in the Wilderness

The Wonder of God's Invigoration

FOREWORD

All of us have submerged currents coursing through our minds — themes, expressions, convictions we return to again and again. Over the years these intra-cranial currents come to characterize how we think and speak, even who we are.

As it has been my privilege to get to know and work with Rev. Dr. Victor Shepherd through his leadership in the renewal movement within the United Church and his editorial contributions to *Fellowship Magazine*, I have noticed several streams of his thinking, speaking, preaching and writing. While they have impressed me with their theological profundity, they have impressed me even more with their cut-to-the-heart, street-value practicality. Those currents are summed up in the title to his book, *Seasons of Grace: from Wilderness to Wonder*.

Here Victor Shepherd ties these four elements together in a marvellous way that speaks to those who may feel bewildered or bruised in a wilderness of any kind, whether personal, career or cosmic — and who believe there is no "escape." Throughout the book he emphasizes that the wilderness is not a situation or circumstance we should seek to escape, but a condition of mind we can find refuge in, even as did our Lord during his earthly journey.

As I considered these four words I wondered about their frequency in Scripture. Pulling out my expanded concordance I began to count the references, assuming "grace" would far out-distance "seasons" or even "wilderness."

Far from it! In all I found 79 versions of "seasons," 181 of "grace," 265 of "wonder" and a whopping 357 "wilderness" mentions — almost one for every day of the year! *Wilderness* is indeed where most of us dwell throughout our entire lives. And the Bible, which ever mirrors reality even in all its unseemliness, doesn't hesitate to state this plainly.

Victor Shepherd will expand your appreciation for *wilderness* and will inspire you to new depths and breadths of *wonder* as you consider the various stages or seasons of grace in your own spiritual life. This book is one you can pick up and read at any chapter, whatever season you find yourself in. And find yourself you will, whether in the doubts of Autumn, the bleakness of Winter, the awakenings of Spring, or the invigoration of Summer. Like the Good Shepherd, the author will lead you to exclaim triumphantly of our God, "He restoreth my soul"!

Whatever the condition or state of your wilderness, may that be your experience as you read on.

Lori E. Gwynne
Editor, Fellowship Magazine

INTRODUCTION

All of us wish life were easier. Troubles afflict us at every turn. They are as abrasive as sandpaper and as relentless as a dripping tap. One day someone dear to us dies, and we are bereaved. Another day disappointment steamrollers us, and we are crushed. The person we always trusted betrays us, and we are flattened. The political climber climbs above us by climbing on us, and we feel we've been buried.

In addition to what befalls us from one day to another there is the chronic affliction whose pain is relentless. One of my friends has a son with cerebral palsy. The son is markedly affected and has never been able to join in children's games and adolescent cavorting. One arm is of little use and one leg drags awkwardly. Recently my friend was waiting for his son, waiting and waiting until his patience curdled into annoyance. "Hurry up!" he shouted in exasperation, not thinking that his son *couldn't* hurry up. To his surprise his son unravelled. "Dad, I am 20 years old; all my I life I have been slow; all my life I've been last. I've constantly heard how I keep people waiting. All my life I've been an impediment, a nuisance, something others endure out of social politeness, secretly wishing they didn't have to." My friend was crushed. The son's affliction is his physical disability; the father's, his guilt over his thoughtless reaction to his son's helplessness.

How much easier it would be to "believe in God" or "take time to be holy" or "sense God's presence" if only we weren't ceaselessly distracted by our troubles!

All of us are stressed in some measure. Yet we all tend to think we're more stressed, more afflicted, more set upon than most. Yes, we admit the human condition extends over humankind. At the same time, nobody quite "knows the trouble I've seen."

Many of us assume our foreparents in faith had an easier time: faith came more readily, life was less harried. They may have suffered more physically (painkillers being unknown), but their mental anguish could never have compared to the emotional torment we're stuck with today.

At the same time we tend to think that in the midst of our intensified suffering we have one enormous advantage over our ancestors: we can *leave* the bleakness of our inner or outer wilderness. Or, if not leave it, at least find relief in ways they could not. We have TA, TM, TV (transactional analysis, transcendental meditation, television). In addition we can "live better chemically," thanks to pharmaceutical companies and their helpful researchers. Whether because of prescription drugs, self-help, psychotherapy or the latest in technological sophistication, we feel that a new era, with new human potential, is just around the corner. One quick turn and the wilderness will be behind us for ever!

Then the truth dawns on us, as discernment is granted to us. *The wilderness belongs to the human condition!* The wilderness is inescapable! To attempt to flee it is to flee life. To try to escape it — and everything about it that chafes us — is to pursue unreality. Here we end up falsifying our humanity, as we magically think we can transcend the human condition. To *succeed* in pursuing unreality tragically lands us in the world of *un*reality: mental illness, derangement, psychosis.

Has God turned his back?

As if our wilderness were not enough, its very bleakness is intensified whenever we suspect, with chilled heart, that God has withdrawn himself from us. We feel he has become deaf or indifferent, that he has turned his back on us. At this point our isolation (part of what it means to live in the wilderness) has worsened into desolation.

The psalmist felt this is what had happened to him. "I commune with my heart in the night," he said in Psalm 77. (Everything seems worse at night!) "I meditate and search my spirit. Will the Lord spurn for ever, and never again be favourable? Are his promises at an end for all time? Has God forgotten to be gracious?" Pouring out his doubts about God, he wondered if God's heart had mysteriously calcified, his steadfast love ceased, his faithfulness to his people evaporated, his promise, "I will never fail you or forsake you," never to be fulfilled.

Further, he was stricken by doubts about himself. "Has God in his anger shut up his compassion?" Everywhere in scripture only one thing arouses God's anger: sin, and only one thing perpetuates it: impenitence in the face of sin. No wonder the psalmist moaned, "I commune with my heart in the night; . . . I search my spirit." Plainly he would have repented instantly if he knew what he had to repent of. But he could only speculate, in his wretchedness, whether, where or how he had sinned so grievously and for how long he unwittingly remained unrepentant.

So confused was he that he wasn't even sure he had sinned at all: "*Has* God in anger shut up his compassion?" How could the psalmist be expected to defuse God's wrath when he didn't even know whether sin-awakened rage was behind God's apparent disappearance?

The wilderness always seems to intensify. It begins with that universal human condition no one can escape and which can only be called a wilderness. Then there is the chilling feeling that God has fallen silent. Finally there is erosion of self-confidence. As the psalmist's self-confidence eroded, he began to spiral down: down into that mess of doubt, self-accusation, depression, short-lived protestation of innocence, longer-lived suspicion of guilt. Left alone he would plummet all the way down to despair.

But just as the psalmist was about to crash a surge of faith short-circuited his doubt. He cried out, "I will call to mind the deeds of the Lord; . . . Thou art the God who workest wonders." His simple recollection of God's feats of old halted the spiral as he particularly recalled the foundational item in his people's consciousness: deliverance through the Red Sea. The Israelites had always believed they were released from slavery in Egypt only because God had taken note of their suffering — in a word, their horrible *wilderness* in the midst of Egypt's luxuriance. The angel of death had passed over them, sparing them annihilation on their way out of Egypt. Were they now to be slaughtered when they arrived at the seaside with no way through? But a way they could never have imagined opened before them. "Thy way was holy," the psalmist exclaimed with gratitude and wonder as he recalled the last-minute deliverance, "Thy way was through the sea, thy path through the great waters."

A way through the wilderness

"Great waters," "seas," "floods" — all these terms in Hebrew symbolize one thing: chaos. Chaos is impenetrable confusion: formless, fathomless, exitless. While there was no way out or around, under God there was a way *through*. "Thy way was through the sea, thy path through the great waters." From that moment Israel exulted ceaselessly in its deliverance.

Then the psalmist added a line all we wilderness-wanderers must hang on to: "Yet God's footprints were unseen." Israel always knew its deliverance to be real, even though God's hand in it remained invisible to others. There was nothing about Israel's deliverance that would dispel unbelievers' unbelief and impel them to cry out, "Truly God *is*!" The literature of the nations that surrounded Israel at this point in history (particularly that of Egypt) contains no reference to the Red Sea event. A rag-tag bunch of social misfits managed somehow to avoid slavery in Egypt? So what! This was nothing to the nations; but to Israel, it was *everything*. To the nations, God's footprints were invisible: God himself appeared unreal. But to Israel, "Thou art the God who workest wonders."

God's footsteps have always been unseen to all except the Spirit-attuned. When the baby was born in the cowshed, who bothered to note one more baby, born out of wedlock, whose arrival could only worsen the poverty of parents who were already poor enough? A few shepherds (and fewer wisemen), however, were overtaken by the wonder of the Incarnate Son who had been appointed Sovereign and Judge of the entire cosmos.

Years later passers-by in Jerusalem saw three crosses on a road leading out of the city. There was nothing noteworthy about them, since Rome had never boasted of either patience or clemency, always preferring to crucify first and ask questions later. Nevertheless, on one cross there hung a young man whose death has ever since found the Spirit-attuned startled at the wonder of their own forgiveness.

City-life continued without interruption in the days after the unexceptional execution. To be sure, members of a small, Jewish messianic sect behaved as if something momentous had occurred.

But Palestine was riddled with small messianic sects that behaved oddly; all one had to do was wait for the sect to sputter out. The story was that some women had taken perfume to the cemetery in order to deodorize a corpse. They were met by him who was the same one they had known for months even as he was now indescribably different.

God's footprints *are* unseen. Yet those in whom the Spirit has surged know that the God "who workest wonders" has come upon them.

Amazement at God's nearness

Wonder is not a sigh of relief as the wilderness is finally left behind. Rather, it is our gasp of amazement at God's drawing near to us in the midst of that wilderness that *cannot* be left behind. While it is true God's footprints are not visible to anyone at all, those who do not harden their heart come to realize that the wilderness is the venue of God's visitation. In this wilderness we're surprised and startled, made to understand and moved to give thanks. Wonder seizes us in the midst of a wilderness we had thought to be as bitter as it is barren. Now we are found exclaiming with the psalmist, "Blessed be the Lord, the God of Israel, who alone does wondrous things" (Psalm 72:18).

As the psalmist reflected on the wondrous deliverance at the Red Sea he realized he could not merely survive in the wilderness, but thrive in it. We too can thrive in our wildernesses as we look to the psalmist and other foreparents in faith. After all, the varied wildernesses that overtook our foreparents were no less bleak or unpromising than ours.

Think of the prophet Hosea. His wife became a prostitute and bore three children whose father could have been anyone except her husband. When she was thoroughly used up, as discardable now as she had long been degraded, she was deemed to have a market value of 15 shekels: half the price of a slave! Absorbing like a blotter the obscene jokes downtown loungers had long snickered over but which Hosea was only now hearing, he made his way to the marketplace and brought his wife home. Why? His love for her was greater than his anguish over her. Thereafter Hosea would speak the warmest word of any Hebrew prophet, steeping his people in God's tenderest love. It's not that Hosea's life-story had a Cinderella-ending. There's no evidence his wife threw herself remorsefully at his feet and lived ever after as his dutiful and faithful spouse. His wilderness was not escaped. But through it, and *only* through it, Hosea was granted the profoundest insight into the wounded heart of God. More, he was entrusted with the tenderest word of God. Through this one man God was able to say to all the people of Israel, "It was I who knew you in the wilderness . . . " (Hosea 13:5). He speaks to all who cringe self-consciously in that wilderness of public humiliation and private shame. They must know they are uniquely qualified to speak gently of a tender love ceaselessly issuing from the God whose people embarrass him but never deflect him.

The still, small voice

Elijah spoke God's truth to political power, to the evil tyranny of King Ahab and his cruel wife, Jezebel. She swore she would kill Elijah. Convinced that faithfulness to God was tantamount to suicide, that his life had boiled dry and might just as well blow away in the desert aridity of it all, Elijah "went a day's journey into the wilderness . . . and asked that he might die" (I Kings 19:4). To his surprise he was fed by a messenger of God. Strengthened now, he made his way to a cave where neither the earthquake, fire nor hurricane bespoke God, while the "still, small voice" — undoubtedly heard by Elijah alone in the wilderness — most certainly did. Told to return home by another wilderness (the wilderness of Damascus: there really is no escape!) Elijah anointed the kings of Syria and Israel, as well as the prophet Elisha, his successor. The wilderness of fear and self-pity is yet the place where we shall know ourselves met, cherished, moved beyond our complaining self-indulgence, and reclaimed for a glad obedience that furthers God's work in the world.

Moses knew his vocation to be that of leader. He also knew hardship in the wilderness was vastly preferable to the security of slavery in Egypt. Through this leader God thundered to Pharaoh, "Let my people go!" Eventually Pharaoh did just that. He would have laughed, however, if he could have overheard the people railing against Moses for 40 years. Life in the wilderness was certainly hard; so hard, in fact, that they clamoured for the "meat, fish, cucumbers, melons, leeks, onions and garlic" of Egypt (forgetting, of course, the wretchedness of the captivity that had reduced them to well-fed domestic animals). Now they were left with nothing better than — manna! "Manna"? The Hebrew word means "What is it?" It's undefinable! The resources of God are unique! They do not fit any of our ready-to-hand categories. What is it? "It is the bread which the Lord has given you to eat" (Exodus 16:15).

The wilderness of leadership

Leadership *anywhere in life* entails loneliness. To be summoned to lead in business, industry, government, church, university, hospital, community organization is to be thrust into a wilderness of loneliness where few others — if any — understand or care.

Yet while Moses is in the wilderness God's fiery presence sets the bush aflame and his scorching truth brands itself upon him indelibly: "Take off your shoes, for the ground on which you stand is holy!" Moses speaks to all who are called to lead and who know the loneliness leadership entails. He tells them faithfulness to their vocation will render their wilderness holy ground. As often as their spirits sag God's fiery presence and word will remind them.

Whenever a leader appears, courage also appears. John the Baptist exemplified courage. His clothing of animal skins gave him an earthy appearance, reflecting the untameability of the wilderness and his aversion to soft compromises. His diet was as stark as his speech: grasshoppers (noted for their protein) and wild honey. (How many bee stings had he incurred in gathering it?) John's courage could come only from someone who was unimpressed by the cute games and politically correct conventions of those who had long since jettisoned transparency. John's fearless truthfulness had found him telling Herod, the puppet-ruler of Judaea, that not even the king had a right to his brother's wife. Royal philandering was still adultery. Herod's sister-in-law (also his mistress) seethed.

Luke tells us John was in the wilderness until his public ministry began. Where was he afterwards? Merely in a wilderness of a different sort. Thirty years in the wilderness for a ministry of only a few months? But what a ministry! The world will never forget the man whom Jesus pointed to as the greatest prophet in Israel. John speaks to courageous people everywhere who discover, sooner or later, that courage brings isolation and calls forth hostility. Just because John didn't flee the wilderness by surrendering courage he continues to embolden all who, like him, will not compromise.

Or consider John's namesake, the seer of the Book of Revelation. This man had been sentenced to spend the rest of his natural life in exile on the island of Patmos. His faithfulness to his Lord in the face of political pressure had landed him on a wind-swept rock-pile as desolate without as John himself was within. Except that he wasn't desolate within! Just because John was stuck on Patmos "on account of the word of God and the testimony of Jesus" the Spirit surged over him, leaving him exclaiming, "I was in the Spirit on the Lord's day."

So far from excluding the Spirit, the wilderness is the condition of the Spirit's visitation. Faithfulness to Jesus Christ in the face of persecution is wilderness to be sure, but also a wilderness where the Spirit unfailingly finds us.

The wilderness surrounds us. The wilderness of shameful humiliation, long-term hardship, isolation enforced because of one's courage, punishment handed out by the politically powerful — it's all *wilderness*. What are we to do when we realize this is where we live and there is no escape? We must look to our foreparents in faith and especially to him who was most at home in the wilderness, Jesus himself.

A place of refreshing

Never attempting to flee the wilderness, our Lord deliberately sought it time and again as a place of spiritual refreshment. He knew life there was spare, hard, even harsh, but he also knew there he'd find fewer distractions, illusions, and the spiritual folly that always attends affluence and its life of ease. Never naive, Jesus knew the wilderness to be the place of temptation, trial and testing. (The Greek word for temptation here, *peirasmos*, has all three English meanings.) At the inception of his public ministry Jesus was even driven into the wilderness, say the gospel-writers in deploying the word used to describe the violent expulsion of demons. (Who says God is always and everywhere gentle?) Yet it was in the wilderness where Jesus was refreshed.

Paradoxically, the place of spiritual assault is also the place of spiritual invigoration. We are sustained most profoundly where we are most threatened! The resources of God abound precisely where we assume they are wanting.

So unusual is this truth that even the most intimate followers of Jesus are slow to grasp it. Jesus drew a huge crowd around himself as he taught for days on end. Matter-of-factly he told the disciples that the crowds, on whom he had stomach-wrenching compassion, needed to be fed. "How can we feed these people in the desert?" the disciples asked, perplexed. They would see shortly that wherever Jesus Christ is present, *anything* offered to him, however slight, is multiplied so as to provide enough for everyone.

We fear the desert or wilderness largely because we assume that whatever desert we are in, for whatever reason, will become even more arid and barren as there is added to it the spectre of spiritual annihilation. The opposite is true. Because Jesus Christ is present the desert becomes the reservoir of riches as indescribable as they are inexhaustible. The prophet Isaiah knew this millennia ago when he wrote, "For waters shall break forth in the wilderness, and streams in the desert" (Isaiah 36:6).

Victor A. Shepherd
Streetsville, Ontario
June 1994

AUTUMN

Hope in the Wilderness

Skepticism dogs us, just as our sinner-state and
suffering threaten to beat us down.
But there is hope in following the One who
prevailed in the wilderness.

Chapter 1

A Good Place to Start

Our spiritual journey often begins with the
question, "Does God exist?"

At first our questions may seem awkward and contrived. But we must shun self-consciousness and start right where we are. As God builds convictions and assurances within us, a peculiar realization occurs: knowing God isn't as crucial as being known by God.

"Does God exist? Does he exist for sure?" There's no single answer that can persuade the doubter or skeptic. No 400-page book will prove, beyond refutation, that God *is*. In fact, there is no irrefutable proof that will convince anyone possessed of elemental logic that God exists.

At the same time, there is no proof that God *doesn't* exist. Sigmund Freud maintained that what people call "God" is simply their wishful thinking projected outside themselves. People believe in God because deep down they want to; they invent God the way a child invents an imaginary playmate. This argument cuts both ways: some simply don't believe in God because they don't want to; they find it convenient not to have God around and so invent his absence the way a child wishes away someone she doesn't like.

There have always been arguments that claimed to prove God's existence, such as the argument from design. If you came upon a wristwatch lying on the sand of a deserted beach, you would have to conclude there was a watchmaker around somewhere. The universe appears to be a grand design; therefore there must be a designer. But of course the question is begged. When we see a watch we already know it's been designed by a watchmaker. But when we look at the universe, we don't know that it's been designed. Eight billion years ago a huge meteor crashed to the earth at Sudbury, Ontario. The force and heat of the impact left lines in the rocks exactly 12 degrees apart, like evenly-spaced wheel-spokes. But we shouldn't speak of a "design" here; it was a random occurrence. No one who doubts the existence of God travels to Sudbury and comes away exclaiming, "Now I really know that God exists!" Other arguments that attempt to prove God's existence never quite prove it.

If we cannot prove God does or doesn't exist, might there be some pointers that incline us in one direction or the other? The evil that scourges people might point to a God *not worth believing in.* A woman once told me of relatives, a husband and wife, who waited for years to have a child. At last she was born. But before long they noticed something peculiar about her eyes. An ophthalmologist told them they were diseased. Before the child was six months old both eyes had been removed.

A pastor from Lithuania visited New York City where he listened to some American ministers discussing their work. The discussion struck the Lithuanian as insufferably shallow. Finally he said quietly, "I was a pastor during the last war. The front surged back and forth through my town eight times. After it had passed each time, all I did was bury people, mostly children."

Most of the world is hungry. In Latin America a handful of very rich people own virtually all the farmland. They use it to grow luxury crops, such as carnations for dining-room table decorations in North American homes. The wretched poor have no access to the land; they're not allowed to grow food for themselves and are paid such a pittance for their semi-slave labour that they cannot afford to purchase the food they need. They remain malnourished and disease-ridden. My cousin went to Honduras as part of a visiting medical team. He found people lining up at the clinic at five o'clock in the morning. All of them were infected and feverish; most had been so for all their lives.

The suffering some people have to endure is simply indescribable. When I was newly-ordained I became friends with a fellow also fresh out of seminary. He had come from a family with 11 children and had gone into debt in order to prepare for the ministry, since his parents couldn't help. He was serving a small congregation which paid the minimum salary, scarcely enough to live on in those days, never mind retire a debt. One evening as he told me how long it would take him to get out of debt (by now he had three children) he wryly remarked to me, "You know, it costs a fortune to be God's witness." Later four inoperable tumours appeared in his head. Does God care a fig for the love, devotion and sacrifice of his servants?

Then perhaps God doesn't exist. At least a God worthy of being loved and adored and obeyed.

If God *isn't*...

But wait! If God simply isn't, then there are sober consequences to be faced.

If God *isn't*, then there is no ultimate redress for human suffering. Those whose lives were afflicted ceaselessly with much less privilege and much greater pain never have it made up to them. Victimized in life, they are cheated still in death. The random loose ends of anyone's life are never gathered up and woven together definitively. Life is just a bagful of loose ends as pointless finally as it is patternless now.

If God *isn't*, then there is no true meaning to life, no transcendent or ultimate meaning. Certainly there can be a meaning to life without God — in fact, a thousand different meanings all the way from what is humanly profound to getting rich through the porn trade or guessing winners at the racetrack. People who pursue these ends find them exceedingly meaningful. But if God isn't, then whatever meaning we find in life is a matter of mere whim.

There is nothing beyond this person's opinion or that person's taste, nothing substantial or finally enduring for us to pursue in life. If God isn't then life ultimately "signifies nothing."

If God *isn't* we can never know what is good just because there is no ultimate good to be known; no good beyond this or that culture's assertion or assessment, someone else's guess or what we hope is good.

If God *isn't* then what is now called "God" is actually mere preference. It may be preceded and followed by reasoning of greater or less rigour, arguments of greater or less cogency, wisdom of greater or less persuasiveness. Nonetheless, at the end of the day, there is no *eternal* good because there is no good that derives its nature from the eternal God himself.

If God *isn't*, finally, then life is a capricious jumble headed for a death whose very deadliness reaches back and begins to deaden life long before we die.

Whether or not God exists there are hard questions to be asked. We find ourselves precisely where the psalmist was when surprised by the Voice: "Be still, and know that I am God!" (Psalm 46: 10). The Hebrew suggests, "Stop being frantic. Stop doing flip-flops in your mind and heart. Just be still for a moment and know — come to know — that I am God."

Even if we *can* be still in this sense, how are we ever going to know that God is God? We have to take *one step forward* in however little faith we have. As we do, we shall find this one step confirmed as a step along the right path — God himself will confirm himself to us as *God*. We then can take a second step, each step granting us greater light until that day when faith gives way to sight and we're bathed in the light of him who is eternal light. On the contrary, each step *not* taken in the littlest light we have means a journey into greater darkness until that day when non-faith gives way to irrecoverable blindness and we're sunk in that blackness our Lord never hesitated to call "outer darkness."

Begin anywhere

What is the first step we should take? There are dozens. Begin anywhere. Begin where conventional "truth of God" seems to collide with the inclination of your own heart. For instance, the Book of Hebrews tells us we must uproot any bitterness in our heart, lest many people become defiled. When next we are kicked or betrayed and have every reason to allow the root of bitterness to thrive, *this time* root it out and see what happens. We'll find we have spared people defilement, including ourselves; we'll have promoted reconciliation and peace — *the* work of God. We'll understand what makes the kingdom of God the kingdom of *God* and how it differs from the kingdoms of this world. Truth and reality will become stamped on us; God will take on a solidity he had always lacked for us.

Having trifled with "Now I lay me down to sleep" for too long, we can resolve to get serious about praying. Either we're going to get serious or we're going to give up the childish recitations as surely as a child ceases thumb-sucking. Start with ten minutes a day wherein we mean business. After a month we shall know perfectly well why Jesus never argued for prayer but simply regarded it as natural and necessary like breathing. Another step along the way is confirmed as truth. And God looms bigger for us.

St. Paul tells us love is not irritable or resentful; neither does it rejoice at wrong. Let's be honest: love is hard work. Kindness pressed upon others without regard for their merit or our recompense is difficult in the face of situations where it's easy to be irritable, resentful or vengeful. Yet as we become "still"; as we dampen down our frenzied irritability and resentment and pursue kindness, we "know," profoundly, the very God whose love for us is a persistent self-giving without regard for our merit or his recompense. As we take even this small step enough light appears for a second step. And then a third.

Several years ago when I visited the Sojourners Community in Washington, D.C., I stayed at the home of Paul and Joanne Sparacio. Raised in an agnostic household, Paul had remained an agnostic throughout his teenage years and young adulthood. He had gone to Viet Nam in the U.S. Army and was in firefights of the sort depicted in *Platoon* or *Apocalypse Now*: phosphorus flares soaring into the air illuminating the battlescene, machine-gun fire, grenade explosions, tracer bullets glowing like laser beams, men screaming in terror and pain. He told us he knew that if he raised himself six inches off the ground he was gone. Eventually he returned to the U.S.A. and enrolled in a southern university, still an agnostic. The students who belonged to the Christian organizations on the campus turned him off utterly. Many who babbled so cavalierly about their beloved Master were racist to the core. They were bent on using religion to reinforce social superiority. Paul told these students he wasn't a Christian, didn't want to be, and that he despised the God they believed in — if such a God there were. Thanks to the Christian students he was no longer an agnostic; he was now a soundly-converted atheist.

Then one day Paul began to suspect, for whatever reason, that these students might have misrepresented Jesus Christ. He avoided them and began reading the New Testament for himself. The Sermon on the Mount arrested him. "Blessed are those who hunger and thirst for righteousness, for they shall be satisfied." He found himself taking that one step. A profound longing, a hunger and thirst he had never been able to put his finger on was identified and met. "Don't be anxious . . . but seek first God's kingdom, and what you have will be enough." The kingdom confirmed itself as truth.

Our first step or two may seem awkward, artificial or even embarrassing to us. But not for long. The day comes when we know with unshakable assurance that God *is* and we are God's child.

Just when we get to this point something peculiar happens to us. We understand that while we do know God, knowing God isn't as crucial as *being known by God*. Being known is always more profound than knowing. When we were little children and felt strange or frightened, our own limited knowledge brought very little comfort. Far more important was the fact that we were known: by our parents, by people we could trust, by those who knew vastly more than we did.

In Psalm 51 the psalmist said he had been searched by God and was now known by God. St. Paul said that regardless of how well we might know God, we are a long way from knowing God fully — even though we are fully known by God right now. God wants only to bless us as our knowledge of him grows surely, however slowly, until that day when we do know fully — as fully as God knows every one of us at this moment.

It all begins with one step.

Chapter 2

COME AND SEE
FOR YOURSELF!

*There's something irresistible about
our Lord's call to us.*

*Persistent doubters
will identify with
Nathaniel who proudly
guarded himself against
gullibility. Yet who
could walk away from one
who knows us as
intimately as Jesus —
and still loves us?*

"Faith is an experiment that results in an experience," preachers used to say 75 years ago. I've never liked the expression. Anyone with even high school training in science knows that experiments are carefully controlled set-ups designed to prove something about nature. But life is not a carefully controlled set-up; therefore it has little in common with laboratory experiments.

What's more, human existence in all its grandeur, depth and wonder cannot be reduced to nature. We do have one foot in the world of nature, but the other foot is in a higher world. We transcend nature in a way that animals do not.

If faith is an "experiment," what is the experience that's supposed to follow it? Some kind of intrapsychic fireworks or ecstasy? I've seen many people, especially youth, urged to "Try

Jesus for the best experience of all." They attempt to work up a religiously-fuelled fervour, never satisfied with the experience they have, always comparing their rather mild feelings to someone else's ecstasies, or to the supposed intense experience they *think* they're supposed to have. Eventually they give up, sadly turning away from the church that has disappointed them, even bitterly denouncing Christian faith as fraudulent.

Any "experiment" in life is going to result in an experience of some kind. Driving an automobile at 200 kph will result in an "experience": either the exhilaration of ultra-high speed, the distress of being arrested and having to forfeit one's driver's licence, or the pain of colliding with a bridge abutment — or worse. The purveyors of street-drugs are quick to tell people that experiments with angel-dust and nose-candy result in a terrific experience.

A cafeteria of options

When we move from the sensational to the apparently profound the problem remains the same. Everyone is faced with a cafeteria of options for believing and living. Christianity is one item, along with the New Age movement, hedonism, nationalism, eastern religions, existentialism and so forth. When people look over the cafeteria-offerings, which are they to select as their experiment? Since all of them result in an experience of some sort, how to choose one over another?

I don't pretend to suggest that saying, "Forget the cafeteria; Jesus is the way to go," is going to persuade many — especially younger people. Then how do people become disciples of our Lord, following him through life 'til death, their conviction growing daily that they've set out on the sure and certain route and should look nowhere else?

We gain insights on how this happens as we look in on our Lord's encounter with Phillip and Nathanael in the first chapter of John's gospel.

Phillip said to Nathanael, his neighbour, "We have found what all of us are looking for — the one who addresses the unspoken longing of our hearts; he is the satisfaction of every thinking person's quest. He is from Nazareth."

"Nazareth!" Nathanael exploded. "Can anything good come out of Nazareth?" Nathanael was plainly sceptical, and there's nothing wrong with this. I'll take sceptics over gullible people any day. The "doubting Thomas," the man or woman from Missouri, is less readily damaged herself and causes less damage.

Gullible people are always being played for suckers. Continually chasing anything that sounds the slightest bit appealing, they're always on the edge of throwing themselves away. They fritter away their time, energy, money, even their innermost substance — their very selves. Again and again they're left jaded, discouraged and embarrassed.

Far better to be sceptical. "Nazareth has never produced anything worthwhile that anyone can recall," was Nathanael's icy reply to Phillip's enthusiasm. "And I don't want to run after this fellow you say you've turned up, only to be left looking like a fool."

Yet scepticism, carried to the extreme, renders us immobilized. If I'm ceaselessly sceptical, not only will I not purchase what is pushed at me through slick advertising, I'll not purchase *anything*. If I'm forever sceptical of the automobile salesperson, I'm going to be stuck with walking everywhere. If I'm sceptical of every last woman, I'll never be married.

If we're to avoid being frozen in 100 percent paralysis, then at some point we have to suspend our scepticism.

Scepticism on hold

How does Nathanael come to suspend his doubts? His friend Phillip says to him, "I know you're a 'doubting Thomas,' but *come and see for yourself*." Nathanael trusts his friend enough to put his own scepticism "on hold" for the moment. Phillip himself had met Jesus on the recommendation of Andrew and Peter. All four men lived in Bethsaida and knew one other. We suspend our scepticism upon the recommendation of someone we trust.

I didn't always think this way. Scepticism was to be hammered out of one's head by rigorous logic. People were to be argued out of unbelief into faith. Now, I don't think faith to be illogical; coming to faith doesn't means pickling one's brains. Nevertheless, to say faith is reasonable is not to say people can be argued into it. Still, I used to think they could be, should be, and I was the one to do it.

When I lived in residence at university and was schooled in philosophy I relished the daily after-supper entertainment. Before serious study got under way for the evening we had to have an intellectual joust. I was good at this. Bold and brazen, I took on all those who argued against faith and slew most of them. Some were easier to argue into silence than others. (Generally it was easier to turn inside out someone from the social sciences than someone from the natural sciences.)

This side of age 50, however, I must say none of the students I hammered intellectually were won to the kingdom (as far as I know). Public defeat did nothing to overcome their scepticism. Instead, their attitude was, "Shepherd, you may have won this round through your verbal footwork, but we aren't impressed and we remain unconvinced as to the truth of what you tell us."

Most people will not be argued out of their unbelief. Then how do they emerge from it? Many different factors work together to bring them to the one Phillip had met and now recommended to Nathanael.

An important factor is our own transparency, our singlemindedness. Upon the recommendation of Phillip, Nathanael started toward Jesus. Our Lord saw him coming and exclaimed, "Here is an Israelite in whom there is no guile" — no deceit, no duplicity. To be honest with oneself, to be without wiliness and cunning is to have taken a giant step towards truth. If at present we believe so little about God that we appear to believe nothing about him, yet are transparent and without duplicity, then we have unknowingly taken a giant step towards faith. To be sincere in one's quest for truth is to find that truth comes forth to meet us. God grants truth to transparency.

Sitting under the fig tree

Another factor in the mix that moves us from unbelief to faith is *sitting under the fig tree.* When Jesus said to Nathanael, "Here is an Israelite as transparent as the day is long," Nathanael replied, "How do you know me?"

"Even before Phillip recommended me to you, I saw you under the fig tree," said Jesus.

It is crucial that we sit, every one of us, under a fig tree. In Israel of old the fig tree was the symbol for the salvation of God. People sat under one when they reflected upon God's redemption. When Jesus said to Nathanael, "I saw you under the fig tree," he meant, "I looked into your heart and saw that deep down you're concerned about the salvation of God and every aspect of it. Your consuming passion is God, his truth, his way, his triumph. I know you long for God's restoration of a world the fall has rendered false and which evil now torments, for his restoration of men and women meant to be his sons and daughters but who live like orphans. I saw you under the fig tree."

At that moment Nathanael cried out, "You *are* the Son of God! You *are* the King of Israel!" At that point his scepticism evaporated completely. He moved from healthy scepticism to healthier faith.

Note: he wasn't argued into faith. He wasn't moved by a barrage that left him unable to reply yet still unconvinced in his heart. Instead several factors moved him: a friend whose recommendation he could trust, his own transparency and sincerity, his concern with matters oceans deeper than baseball scores and interest rates — all these fused together were made fruitful by the approach of Jesus Christ himself. Together they moved Nathanael to become a believer. This is how people continue to become believers today.

Ponder our Lord's promise to his newest disciple: "You will see heaven opened, and the angels ascending and descending upon the Son of Man." Here Jesus brought forward the old story of Jacob who dreamt of angels climbing up and down a ladder that linked heaven and earth. When Jacob awoke he exclaimed, "Surely the Lord is in this place. . . . This is none other than the house of God, and this is the gate of heaven." Jesus adapted Jacob's dream, replacing the ladder with himself: *he* binds heaven to earth and earth to heaven; *he* acquaints us with the essence of God just because he himself *is* the outpoured heart of God and face of God. At the same time he acquaints us with a restored humankind and creation just because he himself *is* this.

All he promises to be

I can say without hesitation or qualification that Jesus Christ is *all* he promises to be.

Jesus Christ is truth. As truth or reality he exposes illusion, fantasy and falsehood for what they are. As I read novels or biographies I do so through the spectacles of God's truth and thereby discern both reality and illusion not only in the characters but in the authors themselves. In turn I'm moved afresh to pursue truth in my own life, repudiating the seductive illusions that always lap at me as surely as they lap at you.

Jesus Christ is life. Since he has been raised from the dead, death *cannot* overtake him; neither can death overtake us who love him.

For years I've been intrigued by a peculiar awareness that looms in 40-year-olds and grows as they age until it becomes haunting: the realization of one's mortality. When someone much older, say 90 or 95, dies, even dies easily, people much younger are disturbed. The person's death has swelled even more their awareness not only of their own mortality, but that of everything about them — children, spouse, parents, careers, savings, aspirations. It's *all* going to be swallowed up in death!

Except! To love him who is resurrection and life is to know two things: first, our coming death is nothing more than mere biological interruption, a momentary disruption of the order of a petty nuisance. Second, everything about us that has reflected the goodness of the kingdom of God will be brought with us through the unavoidable interruption. To say it as clearly as I can: Jesus Christ *alone* is resurrection and life; to love him is to be the eternal beneficiary of what he is in himself.

Jesus Christ is way. The road of discipleship leads us to a glorious destination. The road we walk in faith never winds down into a swamp, a quicksand, a dead-end. Of course it's not always an easy climb. Any suggestion it might be is routed by one reading of the gospels or of John Bunyan's masterpiece, *Pilgrim's Progress*.

Yet as challenging as discipleship is, it will never be greater than the reward. And if in a moment of discouragement we're tempted to think this way is *too* challenging, a quick glance at other roads — meandering, desert-riddled dead-ends — will keep us following him who has pioneered the way ahead of us, accompanies us on the road, and even cheers us on from the finish line where he awaits us.

Twenty centuries ago a man named Phillip said to his friend Nathanael, "I have found someone you should know. Come and see for yourself." Phillip's recommendation inched Nathanael past his scepticism. Nathanael saw for himself, with the result that Jesus Christ became the truth and wonder of his life as well as his eternal destiny.

Come and see for yourself.

Chapter 3

"ALMOST" CHRISTIANS

Before we progress in our faith, we must
ask ourselves what we really believe.

*The gospel inspires
exemplary morality,
beautiful music and
art. But at its core
is a personal
relationship with Jesus
Christ. How can
we cross that threshold
from "almost" Christian
to the "real thing"?*

The church has always been fringed with individuals who seem almost Christian. Sincere, zealous, committed, they appear to be on the cusp of the kingdom. What they're committed to, though, is less than the gospel; for if they were truly committed to Jesus Christ — whose gospel it is — the "almost" would no longer apply.

In the Book of Acts King Agrippa, in response to the apostle Paul's defense of faith before the Roman Governor, says (in the archaic King James language), "Almost thou persuadest me to be a Christian" (26:28). The meaning of the Greek text, however, is actually ambiguous. In the RSV Agrippa says, "In a short time you think to make me a Christian." This suggests not near-persuasion but defiance and a slight mocking: "What makes you think you're going to make a Christian of me?" A better text would be Mark 12:34, where our Lord says to an earnest seeker, "You are not far from the kingdom" (Mark 12:34).

Moralists

Who are "almost" Christians? Moralists who look upon the gospel as a trustworthy guide for personal morality are "not far from the kingdom." They realize that when personal morality is undervalued in a society, chaos results.

Billions of dollars have been poured into the urban jungles of the U.S. with virtually nothing to show for it. Robbery, murder, extortion, drug-trafficking — all these thrive, even proliferate; not to mention the "graft" and indescribable violence. No one seems to know what to do about it.

In Canada it's the same. The last time I was in a criminal court a judge sentenced two 19-year olds who had jammed a knife against the ribs of a Brampton, Ontario teenager and had stolen his Chicago Bulls jacket. "We don't want a society where someone is physically threatened and psychologically traumatized just because he's wearing an item of clothing someone else wants," the judge hissed as he locked up the two fellows. But of course such a society results when personal morality breaks down. Moralists are correct in reminding us what happens when morality is set aside: no one can be trusted. Society crumbles.

In primitive cultures a man had more than one wife. Yet regardless of how many wives he may have had, he *wasn't* permitted another man's wife. Even the most primitive society knew what would happen to the society if wife-raiding were permitted.

Is cheating on examinations a small matter? If we think it is, then we should be prepared to be represented by a lawyer who knows nothing, be operated on by a surgeon who wouldn't know an artery from an eyeball, sold drugs by a pharmacist who is just as likely to poison us, and drive on a bridge whose engineer builds collapsible structures. To say cheating is a small matter is to say professional competence is unimportant. Not only is this ridiculous; it's lethal.

Social improvers

"Almost" Christians are also those who regard the gospel as a program for social improvement. A major factor has certainly been high-quality public education. Egerton Ryerson, the father of Ontario's educational system, envisioned quality public education for *all* children — not merely the sons and daughters of the rich or the established church. It was to be paid for by the taxpayer, since the entire society would benefit.

While realizing the obvious problems with our health-care system, I admire the populist prairie Methodism that eventually gave Saskatchewan quality health care for *everyone*, the remaining provinces soon following its example. Does anyone want to return to the days when hospital bills loomed as the biggest threat to any family? My mother was hospitalized for 75 days with a heart attack. Had she sold everything she owned (and thereafter become a ward of the state) she still couldn't have paid the bills. Does anyone want to suggest quality medical care be available only to the most affluent?

"Almost" Christians recognize it was the gospel that accorded women a place they were denied in ancient Greece and Rome; that it inflamed those who led campaigns on social fronts such as child-labour and working conditions in mines and factories.

Culturalists

"Almost" Christians also include those who recognize the Christian inspiration to art, music and literature. Whenever I walk through an art gallery that features the history of painting I'm startled at the gospel themes depicted: the annunciation to Mary, the boy Jesus "stumping" the clergy in the temple, the crucifixion, the return of the prodigal son. What about Handel's *Messiah*? Mozart's Requiem and Masses, Michaelangelo's sculpture? Consider the gospel themes of countless novels. "Almost" Christians know the gospel has inspired those art-expressions without which we should be humanly impoverished.

In sum, those near the kingdom but not yet in it often skew the gospel by seizing one aspect and identifying the whole gospel with it. As good or moral as it may sound, it's not yet the kingdom, and they're not yet its citizens.

The way "in"

How, then, do "almost" Christians cease being so? First we need to realize that the core, the essence of Christianity is *the living person of Jesus Christ himself*. To be sure, a moral code is useful. We'd all rather have moral neighbours than immoral. Nonetheless, a code, however moral, is qualitatively and categorically different from the living person of the Risen One himself.

We often fail to grasp this because we're misled by the word "believe." In everyday English "believe" means to *admit the truth of a statement*. "Do you believe what you read in the newspaper?" means "Do you admit the truth of the statements in the newspaper?" On the other hand, "Do you believe in Jesus?" means ever so much more than "Do you believe statements about Jesus?" Our Lord didn't first ask people to believe a statement about him, however true; he first asked them to follow him, live with him, love him, trust him. The emphasis is always on *him*, the living person himself — nothing less, nothing other.

The Gospel of Mark indicates that the whole point of our Lord's calling his disciples was "that they might be *with him*." There is no point in addition to this. It's as though someone were to ask, "What's the point in loving one's spouse?" In view of who our spouse is, loving her *is* the point. We're not simply trying to gain something beyond loving her.

"Almost" Christians assume Christianity is somehow helpful or useful. Christians, however, don't think first of usefulness but of *truth*. We know Jesus Christ himself is real; he loves us, longs for us, calls us. Once in his company we realize life with him needs no justification beyond this, just as loving one's spouse is not a means to anything else and needs no further justification.

We move from "almost" to Christian as we come to see that life is ultimately and profoundly not a matter of codes, schemes or artistic inspiration but a matter of *relationships*. Faith is simply a living relationship with Jesus Christ. We enter the kingdom as we enter personally into that relationship with Christ.

Different meanings of the word "faith" can often hinder our becoming Christian. Faith suggests both content and attitude: it can mean the truth to which we subscribe *or* our ongoing trust, love, loyalty and obedience. In our church services recitation of the Apostles' Creed is often prefaced with, "Let us stand and repeat the historic expression of *the faith*." This refers to the ideas or views to which people are asked to subscribe.

Everyone knows, however, that one may subscribe to all the right ideas — even acknowledge them as true — yet possess a heart that is far from God. "This people draw near with their mouth and honour me with their lips," God said through the prophet Isaiah, "while their hearts are far from me and their fear of me is a commandment of men learned by rote." Isaiah's people used correct theological vocabulary but neither feared nor loved God. They had not yet worshipped God because they had never been overwhelmed by him; with nothing written on their heart, they could only regurgitate the "commandment of men." The apostle James says devils espouse an impeccable, entirely orthodox theology; nevertheless, they remain devils.

Someone who subscribes to every last item in the Apostles' Creed is said to possess strong faith, while someone who can't is said to possess weaker faith. The truth is, both could possess no faith at all: they could subscribe to right ideas yet have no trust in our Lord.

We move from "almost" to "Christian" as we come to love, honour, trust, fear, thank and obey our Lord. We commit *as much of ourselves as we know of ourselves* to *as much of him as we know of him*. If we have reservations about some orthodox expressions of Christian belief, we can wait to have them dealt with; but we cannot and *must not* wait to commit ourselves to God.

Jesus maintained that obedience was a major distinction between pseudo-disciples and genuine disciples. With both exasperation and grief Jesus says to would-be disciples, "Why do you call me, 'Lord, Lord,' and not *do* what I tell you?" Then he immediately relates the parable of the man who built his house on rock (the house surviving a flood, the biblical symbol for chaos) and another who built his house on sand (the house collapsing into ruin). His point is clear: obedience spells the difference between thriving and dying.

The one key of life

George MacDonald, nineteenth-century Scottish writer, said, "obedience is the one key of life." This should be etched into our minds forever. "Whoever will *live* [that is, truly live] must cease to be a slave and become a child of God. There is no halfway house of rest where ungodliness may be dallied with, nor prove quite fatal."

When a young man complained he didn't understand some of Jesus' commands, MacDonald commented, "Had he *done* as the Master told him, he would soon have come to understand. Obedience is the opener of eyes . . . It is simply absurd to say you believe or ever want to believe him, if you do not *do* anything he tells you . . . To say we might disobey and be none the worse would be to say that *no* might be *yes* and light sometimes darkness."

We move finally and assuredly from "almost" to "Christian" when our obedience goes to the lengths Jesus himself speaks of when he says, *If anyone wants to be mine, let him, let her, take up her cross and follow me.* The sign that our following is sincere, whole-hearted and not merely a romp or a picnic is the crossbearing it entails; when there is genuine sacrifice we gladly make for him who first sacrificed everything for us.

At this point the "almost" Christian has become "the real thing." Indescribable joy erupts in heaven, not to mention the joy in the individual's heart.

Chapter 4

HELP FOR OUR HALF BELIEF

Spiritual misfits that we are, we can only see our way by acknowledging our blindness.

The epileptic boy drew a crowd; so do our modern church controversies. But just as the boy's disfiguring ailment ultimately points to a deeper spiritual problem besetting humankind, so must our sinner-state lead us to kneel before him who alone can make our faith whole.

Controversy has been unavoidable in the church in any era. Peter tells us in his first letter that we should always be ready to articulate our gospel-convictions when challenged. Time after time, on his missionary journeys, Paul went to the marketplace or a church-hall and argued for the truth and substance of the faith. This isn't to say that he argued nastily, became contemptuous or sarcastic. But he was prepared to speak up for the gospel of God whenever it was maligned, distorted or simply misunderstood.

As the gospel has been contradicted in our day some of us have had to speak up, argue and dispute — all in a manner that adorned the gospel itself. As we have done this a crowd has gathered.

God has ordained that there be a place for this. *Dialogizomai* is a rich New Testament word meaning to dialogue, question, contend. Yet arguing and reasoning with respect to the gospel are never ends in themselves. Paul didn't argue in the marketplace because he relished defeating someone in a verbal joust. He argued only for the sake of the gospel. We do as much today only in order to dispel misunderstandings of the gospel, to clear away obscurities that might be impeding faith in our hearers. Ultimately our purpose is to get beyond argumentation and have others embrace the gospel itself.

In the ninth chapter of Mark we find the disciples of Jesus arguing with the scribes. We understand why they must. Loving controversies, a crowd has gathered. Yet as soon as Jesus showed up the crowds forgot the arguing and flocked around him. They did so, Mark tells us, because they were amazed at him; as soon as they saw him they were startled at the authority he exuded. They recognized he could do for them what no one else could.

One of the crowd had brought his ill son to the disciples. He assumed that where there are disciples of Jesus there is also the power of Jesus. As soon as Jesus appeared the parent recognized that *this* man was the one he was really looking for.

Why people come to church

People from "the crowd" come to our churches. Some seek answers to theological dilemmas. Some have recently become parents and are sobered by their new responsibility. Others have lost someone dear to them and have questions they cannot answer and a heartache they cannot assuage. People come to our churches after any one of life's countless jarrings have left them wondering profoundly or wobbling drunkenly. In coming into the midst of those of us who are disciples of Jesus, they assume they are drawing near to Jesus himself, that from the midst of Christ's people there will be given them what they need, or at least what they're looking for and what our Lord alone can supply.

Sometimes they come only to go, feeling that what they expected to find isn't there. Others, however, remain long enough that our Lord himself appears to them. In that instant, like the crowd, they recognize that *he* is the one with authority. They're startled as they recognize what they cannot put words to, yet *know*. Whether they've been attracted by the controversial edge of some churches or put off by it, they realize disputes were never ends in themselves but for the sake of the one who has loomed before them and whom they know to love them.

The human condition

When the anguished father brought his son to Jesus, the boy went rigid; he convulsed and foamed. Plainly he was epileptic.

The ailments brought to Jesus during his earthly ministry were certainly distressing ailments in themselves, but they were also signs of a deeper, more difficult spiritual problem besetting humankind. Blindness is a dreadful affliction. To be deprived of sight is certainly to be victimized by evil. Since Jesus resisted evil wherever he came upon it, he restored sight to those who were blind.

Blindness is also symbolic of humankind's spiritual condition, as the New Testament stories point out starkly. We are blind to the nature and purpose of God, to the signs of God's presence, to the truth about ourselves and to our situation before God, the just judge.

When Jesus restored sight to the physically blind, he expanded the meaning of his action to include the spiritual blindness that afflicts us all. In the account of our Lord's meeting with Nicodemus Jesus said to him, "Truly, unless one is born anew [born of God] one cannot even *see* the kingdom of God, much less enter it." Only as the truth and power of God penetrate us do we become spiritually perceptive and discerning.

Similarly, the symptoms of the boy's epilepsy point to symptoms of our spiritual condition.

First, the boy is dumb, mute; can't speak at all. Humankind does not praise God. This is startling, since we are commanded to praise God (the most frequently repeated command in scripture). The primary characteristic of God is that he speaks: he speaks *to* us in expectation of eliciting speech *from* us. The absence of heartfelt and heartmeant exclamation to God is spiritual dumbness. Only as there is a restorative work of God within us are we freed to praise God from our heart.

Second, the boy's behaviour renders him unsightly and self-destructive. A seizure never yet made anyone beautiful; neither does our sin render us attractive. Our spiritual condition, of course, is what underlies those unsightly outcroppings we call sins. We don't pretend for a minute that they produced themselves. They're symptomatic of a spiritual condition deep in us, hidden to all except those with Spirit-quickened understanding. Still, the outcroppings are what everyone sees, whether believer or unbeliever.

No list of sins could ever be complete, since our underlying sinnership effervesces inexhaustibly. Nevertheless, here and there in scripture we come upon partial lists. When Jesus speaks of our root condition of sinnership and refers to its outcroppings he speaks off the top of his head of "evil thoughts, fornication, theft, murder, adultery, coveting, wickedness, deceit, licentiousness, envy, slander, pride, foolishness." He stops there only because he assumes he has made his point. In the same way Paul rattles off "covetousness, malice, envy, murder, strife, deceit, gossip, slander, hatred of God, insolence, abuse of parents, foolishness, faithlessness, heartlessness, ruthlessness" — until he has run out of breath. Any one of us could add another 50.

Self-destruction

The boy's behaviour also renders him self-destructive: his affliction has often thrown him into water and fire. Sin is humanly destructive. Sin slays, to be sure, and it issues ultimately in spiritual annihilation. This too is part of the human condition.

Third, when the boy's father is asked how long his son has been afflicted, he blurts out, "He's been like this from childhood!" I know for how long I've been afflicted with my sinnership, and for how long you've been afflicted with yours: from childhood.

Our Lord's depiction of the human condition is accurate. Few people, however, believe him. They're convinced that education, the welfare state, improved recreational facilities, better health care will together transmute the human condition. It won't. Only the touch of our Lord does this.

The father brought his boy to Jesus and said, "If you can do something, anything, have pity on us and do it."

"Do you believe that I can?" asked Jesus, "or are you simply giving utterance to a bit of wistful thinking?"

"I *do* believe you can," the man said, "but I can't seem to believe enough! Do something about my unbelief!" Jesus then restored the boy to health.

You and I are no different. We do believe our Lord is saviour. We're not dabbling in wistful thinking. We do believe he alone can deal with our sinnership. Yet when we search our hearts, look out onto the world, note what awaits us, then look back into our hearts, we're like Peter getting out of the boat with a modicum of confidence only to look at the waves around him and find himself going under. Every time we say, "I believe," we're also driven to cry, "but I can't seem to believe enough!"

To say this, however, is to admit we cannot generate faith ourselves. We cannot possess greater faith by fostering or facilitating something inside our psyches. There is no incantation, meditative technique, guru-gimmick or mystical magic by which we can generate faith out of our own resources. We come to possess greater faith only by looking away from ourselves and our half-believing hearts to the God who has promised to enlarge even mustard-seed faith. We must keep on looking to him, for only then will we be fully assured our Lord can restore us and will restore others.

A matter of prayer

The disciples, who witnessed the restoration of the boy, were taken aback at their own spiritual impotence. The boy's father had brought him to the disciples assuming they were possessed of the very thing their master exemplified and lends to his followers. Sobered, the disciples could not deny their own spiritual poverty. "Why do we appear ineffective in the face of humankind's condition and need?" they asked. Jesus replied tersely, "It's a matter of prayer; always a matter of prayer."

Here our Lord doesn't mean muttering a religious formula but petitioning God morning and night to magnify the faith he has given us. It's a matter of exercising the faith we have by concentrating more on the risen one who stands in our midst than on the turbulence that forever laps at our lives. It is contending for the truth of the gospel (as we must) without crushing ourselves by thinking the future of God's kingdom hinges on the success of our argumentation. It is acknowledging that we share in Christ's victory only as we participate in his sufferings.

Prayer is always a matter of not fleeing or cluttering the wilderness-episodes of our lives but recognizing that we're led into them in order that we, like Jesus before us, might hear our Father speaking to us with new clarity. All of this was gathered up as Jesus said to the disciples, "Spiritual authenticity is found in those who pray."

Mark's account here of a disordered, disfigured fellow typifies not only the root human condition but also that work of grace by which our Lord renders you and me creatures who redound to the praise of God's mercy, even as the same grace renders our insufficient belief sufficient unto that day when faith will give way to sight and we shall behold our blessed Lord face-to-face, forever and ever.

AUTUMN

The Wonder of God's Grace

God's grace keeps us. Regardless of how we may feel
through the seasons of life, God's image of us in Christ
is the lens through which he sees us. This is the
final truth about us all.

Chapter 5

WE ARE A "KEPT" PEOPLE

God preserves and safeguards us in the wilderness.

Where do we go for help? Escape to the hills, or into culture, politics or even rugged individualism won't help. God alone keeps us — not cushions us — in our going out and coming in.

Mountains are beautiful: majestic, imposing, immovable. Therefore it's easy to assume we know what the psalmist means when he cries, "I lift up my eyes to the hills." Actually, he doesn't mean what we think he means, since mountains were ambivalent for the Israelite people: awesome to be sure, yet also a source of danger. Outlaws and cutthroats hid in the mountains and swept down out of the hills to harm travelers. The mountains themselves were treacherous for voyagers, riddled with gorges, precipices and wild animals.

We modern folk like to imagine mountains (indeed, all of nature) as relief from burnout and as a source of refreshment. The ancient Israelites knew better. In Psalm 11 the psalmist was tempted to "flee like a bird to the mountains" where he could get away from it all. But he knew not even birds were safe in the mountains: food was exceedingly scarce among rocks and predators abounded. For this reason as soon as the psalmist looked at the distant mountains and asked, "From whence does my help come?" he answered, "My help comes from the Lord," from Yahweh. Ultimately help does not come from the mountains, from nature; the profoundest help we need comes from God the maker of heaven and earth.

Nevertheless this lesson is not learned quickly. In an increasingly secularized age help is sought from every quarter except the Lord. Yet the places we look to for help are like the mountains: attractive, beckoning, with much about them that is genuinely good, yet also threatening and ultimately not helpful in the profoundest sense.

As noted, culture, good or bad, can never penetrate as deeply as we need to be penetrated; it cannot finally "keep" us in the sense in which the Lord our God is our keeper. Neither can the state. In a fallen creation, of course, the state is *always* ambivalent and double-edged. Meant for blessing, it in fact curses millions. It would be difficult to convince masses in the world right now that the state is their helper in any sense.

Then there are rugged individualists, brimming with confidence, who argue that one's psychological resources are sufficient. Make no mistake: our inner resources *are* wonderful. I marvel at what people have in them: intuition, coping-mechanisms, resilience, creativity.

But hidden in everyone's intrapsychic landscape are psychological booby-traps. All of us have dark recesses in our psyche that startle us when we least expect it just because we never guessed — couldn't guess — what lurks within us.

The psalmist, then, is correct. While he's tempted to flee to the mountains and seek help there, he knows that the mountains, though beautiful and dangerous, cannot provide the kind of help he most profoundly needs. The same must be said of anything else we think might profoundly help.

What do we need?

Our help comes from the Lord. But what kind of "help" do we need? We aren't so foolish to assume we are promised divine assistance for our pet projects, or worse, for our ambition or avarice. God is not the rocket fuel that powers whatever we think will let us "get ahead." Then what is the nature of the help we both need and crave?

This is answered by the psalmist's repeated use of "keep" and "keeper": *We need to be "kept," preserved, safeguarded.* At bottom we know we need one thing above all else: we need the identity God has given us in Christ to be safeguarded and preserved in the midst of everything that threatens in life, as well as in death. We know we can't avoid sickness, setback and suffering. No one is spared these. What we want, deepest down, is for the real me, what I am in Christ — the "me" that is so profound God alone sees and knows it — to be safeguarded *now* so as to be kept *forever*. Paul tells believers in Colosse that their ultimate identity is hid with Christ in God. What we most profoundly need is for what is *hid* with Christ in God to be *kept* with Christ in God until that day when nothing will be able to assail, crumble or evaporate it.

I have long been intrigued by the answers different people give to the question, "Who tells you who you are?" The question is significant because our answers *determine* who we are. Do my parents tell me who I am? To some extent, but if they alone do then I've never grown up. Does my academic achievement, professional standing or reputation tell me who I am? These can only give me the most artificial identity. Do *I* tell myself who I am? This can result in a most confusing identity, since the "I" who tells the "I" who is told is like trying to set a watch to a factory whistle while trying to set the whistle to the watch. Who tells any of us who we are? And after whoever or whatever makes us who we are, who or what is going to "keep" us in the psalmist's sense of "keep"?

The keeper of Israel

The One who keeps us is the One who has kept Israel. He "made" Israel, a people ordained to live for the praise of his glory and the enlightening of the nations. Having fashioned them he has kept them. When they were threatened with dissolution in Egypt or discouraged in the wilderness, when prophets were dismayed at the faithlessness of the people — still the holy One of Israel kept them.

The psalmist argued that since God has so manifestly kept

Israel, the people, God can be trusted to keep every person who is individually a member of Israel. Because the God who kept Israel has promised to keep the Church so that not even the powers of death can prevail against it, he will surely keep us who are members of it.

From the formation of Israel to the birth of Jesus 1,300 years elapsed. Israel was kept. The day came when Israel was gathered up into the person of Israel's greater Son. Was *he* kept? Apparently not! Yet as he was raised from the dead and made to live forever he *is* kept — his people with him, and us with his people. He who keeps Israel and his heirs neither slumbers nor sleeps. There will be no forgetful or careless lapse on God's part during which something from within or without us might deprive us of our identity before God or our security in him.

Sunstroke

Against what has God promised to safeguard us? Against the sun and the moon, says the psalmist. The sun shall not smite us by day nor the moon by night. We laugh, even snicker, at this. Who gets sunstroked today? And even if travelers in hot countries might get sunstroked from time to time, who ever got moonstroked?

But we shouldn't laugh. To our Hebrew foreparents the sun symbolized overwhelming perils on life's journey. To be "sunstroked," metaphorically, was to be "done in" by developments that were part and parcel of the journey itself. Don't we speak metaphorically today of being "burnt out"? When we come upon someone who is manifestly "burnt out" we don't rush her to the hospital for a skin graft! We mean that ordinary, day-to-day developments have become too much for her.

Employment is an everyday aspect of life's journey. Having a job, having to work, isn't extraordinary. Yet work can leave people burnt out. Parenting is a normal part of life's journey. Yet in some circumstances parenting would leave anyone beside himself. (If ever you are tempted to think otherwise, come with me to family court for one day.) Having aged parents isn't unusual. Yet the stress of dealing with elderly parents can collapse us.

When the psalmist insisted we're going to be "kept" he didn't mean we're going to be cushioned. Any Christian who expects to be cushioned should look more closely at the Master himself. Was he cushioned — against anything? Yet he was ultimately kept against everything, for no development left him devoid of his identity before his Father. What caused him to sweat so profusely in Gethsemane that it poured off his face like blood from a forehead gash; what caused him to cry out, "Even my Father has abandoned me!" — none of this ultimately dissolved him. It was all an occasion in which his Father "kept" him, safeguarded him, preserved his identity, even as he felt it not.

We are not cushioned; we are kept. Our identity and security before God are safeguarded regardless of day-to-day developments that appear to overwhelm us on life's journey.

Moonstroke

Moonstroke is something else. The ancient world believed the moon gave off noxious powers, among which were diseases of all kinds. Disease is rooted in micro-organisms we cannot see: tiny, yet insidious and dangerous. Whereas to be "sunstroked" is to fall victim to what overwhelms us frontally on our journey, to be "moonstroked" is to be submarined insidiously by what we do not see, cannot foresee, and against which we're not forearmed.

When I was studying in Scotland I preached one Sunday at an Anglican church. One of the families invited the Shepherds home for lunch. Our host and hostess were both physicians. They were telling us of a clergyman who was transparent to the gospel, who had had inestimable influence upon them, and who had meant the world to them. At the height of his powers this clergyman had come down with encephalitis, was severely brain-damaged, and could only babble, slobber and stumble. So overcome was my host in recounting his sad tale that he stopped speaking. Feeling awkward at the silence I admitted my medical ignorance and asked him how his friend had come to have encephalitis. My host turned to me and said slowly and sadly, "How does anyone get it?" He meant, "Isn't it tragic that we can be contending triumphantly with developments in front of us (sunstroke won't get us) when unbeknown to us something insidious can submarine us and reduce us to a pitiable creature!" If my host had lived 3,000 years ago he would have said, "My clergyman-friend appears moonstroked!"

Dr. Oliver Sacks, whose work inspired the movie *Awakenings,* spent much of his time with patients whose Parkinsonian symptoms were rooted in encephalitis. Where others saw human wreckage so wrecked as to be subhuman, Sacks saw creatures of God whom God "kept" despite the ravages of their disease. Even the people who gave greatest evidence of being moonstroked ultimately were not!

God will not cushion me against encephalitis. (He who did not cushion that Son with whom he is ever pleased is not going to cushion me.) But he will keep me — ultimately — against sunstroke and moonstroke alike. Who I am in Jesus Christ, who I really am even though I myself only glimpse it from time to time — *this* is what God will safeguard and keep regardless of what may seem to have overwhelmed me frontally or submarined me insidiously.

The scope of God's keeping

If the nature of God's safeguarding is to preserve me against sunstroke and moonstroke, what is the scope of God's keeping? The psalmist says God can be trusted to keep my "going out and my coming in." This is a rich Hebrew expression with three distinct meanings.

It is a Hebrew way of expressing totality or entirety, a way of saying *everything.* To say God will keep our going out and our coming in is to say nothing that befalls us will ever undo God's keeping. Nothing will ever handcuff God so as to leave him unable to keep us. He who was not handcuffed by the death of his Son is not going to be handcuffed now.

It refers to the important ventures, efforts and undertakings of life. To have these "kept" is to have our worthwhile efforts rendered fruitful. Psalm 126 promises, "He who goes out weeping, bearing the seed for sowing, shall come in with shouts of joy, bringing his sheaves with him." To know God will keep our going out and our coming in is to know that our worthwhile undertakings in life — into which we have poured ourselves — are not going to be fruitless finally. We may have seen little fruit to date for the energy we have poured out, the sacrifice we have made and the prayers we have pleaded; nonetheless, it all isn't finally going to dribble away! It's going to be crowned.

"Going out and coming in" refers to the early and sunset years of life, infancy and old age, when we are helpless. At the beginning of life and at the end we are kept. The child who dies in infancy, even the still-born child (not to mention the aborted child) is kept inviolate before God, by God. The most senile person in the nursing home whose befuddlement has left him virtually unrecognizable; this person is kept before God as well.

My heart rejoices that the God who neither slumbers nor sleeps will keep my going out and my coming in. For as often as I may lift up my eyes to the hills, I know my help comes not from the hills but from the Lord. He will keep me in the face of sunstroke and moonstroke alike, from this time forth and for evermore.

Chapter 6

COMFORT FOR EAGLE NESTERS

God's people in exile today often feel wilderness-weary,
but we can find comfort where we dwell.

When we feel exiled in an increasingly secularized age, we can find relief in waiting on the Lord. Because Christians live in places accessible only to those born of the Spirit, there is encouragement and safety only other eagle-nesters can give.

Do you ever feel like an alien in Canada even though you may have lived here most or all of your life? Has the current culture exiled you, left you feeling you don't belong any longer?

One of my friends, a vice-principal in Scarborough, was telling a grade-eight class about the popular musical, *Joseph and the Amazing Technicolour Dreamcoat.* Not one child knew it was based on a biblical story. Amazed, my friend took his discovery to the staffroom. Not one of his fellow-teachers knew of its Bible origins either.

With the erosion of the Judaeo-Christian tradition my friend has observed the decline of other qualities we've long taken for granted: punctuality, honesty, diligence. One grade-eight youngster came to school late, sat down sulkily and informed the teacher he was going to do no work at all. He wouldn't open a book, pick up a pen, or think a thought. He was determined to do nothing except frustrate the teacher and encourage other students to follow him in his defiance. When my friend informed the boy's mother that her son was going to be suspended, the mother accused my friend of picking on her boy: "Why? He hasn't done anything wrong. He doesn't have to do schoolwork if he doesn't feel like it."

I often feel like an exile, an alien, a stranger forever out-of-step. In the wake of mushrooming AIDS in India an epidemiologist there has concluded that all government attempts at informing people of the ways, means and consequences of infection are utterly useless. Only one thing has any chance of bringing people to their senses, says this M.D., and that is *fear*. By this he means *sheer terror*. The AIDS picture is to be painted so horrifically that people will be terrified.

It's odd that often when ministers say God is to be feared they've been accused of emotional blackmail, manipulation, psychological assault. We're not permitted to say God is to be feared even though what's at stake is nothing less than our eternal well-being. We are permitted, however — even urged — to say AIDS is to be feared when what's at stake is our *temporal* longevity. Where salvation is the issue, fear is deemed deplorable; where infectious disease is the issue, fear is deemed commendable. Am I in exile? I must be living on another planet!

I am amused when I read the rhetoric spouted by boards of education concerning pluralism. It appears that the Christian faith (which, to say the least, is undeniably a major factor in Canada's historical formation and cultural richness) has been muzzled on the grounds that it is religion, while non-Christian religions are given place and voice on the grounds that they are part of the new cultural mosaic. Informing students of the significance of Christmas and Easter is unacceptable, while acquainting them with the other religious festivals is educational. Do you ever feel yourself an alien precisely where you used to think you belonged?

There are other reasons we often feel exiled. People don't feel "at home" with life-in-general, with themselves, ultimately with God, because too many negativities have piled up too quickly. Recently I've attempted to support a family whose mother has had to undergo very extensive surgery for life-threatening disease. Her husband is on permanent long term disability benefits, having undergone a head-injury in an automobile accident that left him chronically impaired.

Not so long ago I interviewed a couple who wished to get married. As always I asked if either had been married before. The fellow had. Assuming he was divorced I asked if he had the required papers. Quietly the man said, "I'm a widower. My wife died of a brain hemorrhage. I have one child, a boy fifteen, and he has Down's Syndrome." I understand if these people and others may sometimes feel exiled and long to feel "at home."

Unsearchable understanding

The first 39 chapters of the book called Isaiah were written by a prophet who lived 800 years before our Lord. The remaining chapters were written 200 years later, during the Babylonian exile, by an unnamed prophet or school of prophets. The Israelite people had been carried off into exile. Their captors, the Babylonians, taunted and despised them. The Israelites felt so far from home they couldn't feel stranger. Compounding their aloneness in the midst of the Babylonians was their feeling that God had abandoned them. It's bad enough to be a non-citizen in a land where you don't belong and have no rights; how much worse also to endure the haunting impression that God has forgotten you.

They couldn't help asking themselves, "Will anything ever jog God's memory? Will he ever return to us?" The Israelite people knew they had been appointed a light to the nations. Yet most of the time they now groped in the dark themselves. All too soon they became dispirited, demoralized, weary. Why not give up and yield to the pressure of Babylonian paganism? They were weary beyond telling.

I understand because I know how weary God's people in exile feel today. But to the weary people of the world Isaiah cries,

Have you not known? Have you not heard?
The LORD is the everlasting God.
He does not faint or grow weary.
His understanding is unsearchable. (Isaiah 40:28)

This prophet doesn't begin by patronizing his people, "Cheer up now, nothing is as bad as it appears." He doesn't insult them by reminding them they'd feel better if only they stopped bellyaching. Instead he directs their attention away from themselves to God. "Do you not know? *He* doesn't grow weary, ever. And his understanding is unsearchable."

God's grasp of our situation is wider, deeper, more comprehensive than our fragmentary, distorted grasp can ever be. It's as though we have our faces pressed up against a beautiful painting: huge, cohesive, not in the least cluttered or chaotic. But we're so close to the welter of detail that we can't even recognize it; it looks to us like a smudge, a smear, a blot that means nothing.

Or imagine yourself looking up at the underside of a rug. You can see splashes of colour, bits of this and that, unaccounted-for threads dangling here and there. If we could only see from above we'd realize the million-and-one threads have been formed into a pattern that is nothing less than breathtaking.

God's understanding is unsearchable. As the weaver, God sees what he weaves. For the time being we can see only the underside and must trust him with the topside. For not only is his understanding unfathomable, his persistence is undeflectable just because *he never grows weary*. The prophet comforts his people not by pretending exile is less onerous than they know it to be but by directing them to the God who comprehends their situation now and will weave something glorious from it which they will see for themselves one day and for which they will praise him.

No loitering

In the meantime, says this unnamed prophet, we are to *wait for the Lord*. Not wait around, linger aimlessly or loiter mindlessly; we are to set our hope on him and entrust our future to him. We are to hang on to him for the present and wait for him for the future. He can weave something glorious from that jumble of irruptions which currently leaves us agape if not aghast. He can comprehend at once in his "eternal now" what we see only piecemeal with each fragmentary instant. Not even those developments in our lives that we perceive as unrelieved negativity are going to frustrate him. *Then wait for him we must.*

Yet even as we wait for him we do not find ourselves waiting around, nothing going on. Eversomuch is going on since, says the prophet, as we wait for him our strength is renewed; we run without giving up in weariness and we walk without falling down faint.

Those who wait for the Lord shall renew their strength. Believers of every era have found God to be as good as his promise. Centuries before the prophet wrote this text Joshua spoke God's message to a fearful people: "Be strong and of good courage; be not frightened, neither be dismayed; for the Lord your God is with you wherever you go."

Covered promises

"Be strong! Be of good courage!" It's a command, not a promise. Nevertheless, the spiritual giants of Puritanism used to say, "All God's commands are covered promises." Every directive of God is a veiled promise of God. Regardless of what God commands us to do, he first promises us the wherewithal to do it. It is the command of God that we be strong; it is the promise of God that if we wait for him we shall find our strength renewed.

Believers without number can testify that God has fulfilled this promise time and again in their lives. For our own encouragement we should listen to the testimony of others, such as the impoverished, sick woman whom Jean Vanier was visiting in the slums of Cleveland. He was taken aback at this woman's medical condition, startled by her economic condition, and didn't know what comfort to offer. Finally, perplexed, he simply placed his hand on her forehead and said, "Jesus."

"I been walking with him 40 years," she whispered.

Years earlier John Paton, missionary to the pacific island of Tonga, went with his wife on the mission field knowing that God had commissioned them both to this ministry. Shortly after arriving on the island he had to bury his wife, followed by his daughter a few days later. He wrote in his journal there were moments when he felt he was on the edge of irremedial blackness, yet always came to know afresh that he was sustained, strengthened for that vocation which he also knew had *not been rescinded.*

The apostle Paul said, "I have learned to be content, whatever the circumstances may be. I know how to live when things are difficult and how to live when things are prosperous . . . . I have learned the secret of eating well or going hungry, of facing either plenty or poverty. *I am ready for anything through the strength of the one who lives within me"* (Philippians 4: 12-13).

Six hundred years before Paul wrote this, his ancestors, powerless in the face of the Babylonian captivity and exile, had also proved the promise. Just because they waited for God and were strengthened they were able to live — not pine, whine or decline — but thrive, even in the wilderness of exile.

Where eagles live

Those who wait for the Lord will mount up with wings like eagles. Our Hebrew foreparents had noted that the eagle nested in inaccessible places where only other eagles lived. Only fellow-believers know where I live, because only they *can* live where I live.

There is a profound sense in which the Christian lives in an inaccessible place. He or she lives where those not yet born of the Spirit do not live simply because the kingdom of God is accessible only to those born of the Spirit. There is a struggle peculiar to the Christian only other Christians know about, as well as a comfort only they can give, just because only they profoundly have access to us.

I cannot tell you how often I've been helped by the spiritually sensitive who know the frustrations, discouragements and occasional clobbering peculiar to a minister — and who have lent me the comfort, encouragement and even safety only other eagle-nesters can. Christians who are in assorted exiles in our secularized, pluralistic age know that to wait for the Lord is to comfort others and be comforted ourselves with a balm uniquely ours in the midst of our difficulty.

Those who wait for the Lord are going to run without becoming weary; so weary, that is, as to quit running. In the ancient Hebrew world jogging was unheard of and the Olympic Games centuries away. People never ran for leisure. They ran for two serious reasons: to deliver good news and to save life. Both purposes coalesce in the gospel, for the gospel is good news that also saves.

However much you and I may feel alienated in our culture, exiled in a milieu that disdains hard-edged truth and prefers sentimental illusion, we remain charged with the responsibility of running without growing weary to the point of not running. We must exemplify and commend that good news which, vivified by God himself, saves from death, destruction and damnation. The fact that the gospel seems to evaporate before it has chance to soak in is not our responsibility. The hearing it receives in an alien culture is not our burden. All that matters is that we continue to exemplify and commend what we know to have brought us life in God. The prophet tells us that as we wait for the Lord we shall continue to do just this.

Against the flow

Moreover, those who wait for the Lord are going to walk and not faint or collapse. Walking is the commonest Hebrew metaphor for obedience. Throughout scripture we are told to walk worthily of God and our calling, to walk as children of light in newness of life. Our walk is simply the ethical shape faith lends our lives. To walk worthily is to obey him who insists that where there is no obedience there is no faith, even as he insists that the gate that admits us to the walk is narrow and the walk itself rigorous. Discipleship is not a cakewalk, not a saunter; it doesn't meander. Above all, the walk of discipleship is always and everywhere walking *against the flow* of the shufflers and strollers and dawdlers all around us.

When my wife caught a grade four girl stealing Explorer money out of our home in Toronto the girl's mother exclaimed, "Why was my daughter so stupid as to let herself be caught?" Plainly the disparity between what God requires of his people in all areas of life and what our society endorses is immense. It was disturbing when university students regularly approached me for essays they could crib and turn in as their own for an "A" grade when in fact they were ignorant, lazy, dishonest and soon to occupy pulpits, class-rooms or law offices.

The one thing about the Israelites that first amazed but then angered their Babylonian captors was their refusal to capitulate. They told their Babylonian exilers straight out, "If we conform to you outwardly we'll not know who we are inwardly, for in fact we shall have ceased to be God's people."

To walk without fainting means that you and I are going to behave as followers of Jesus without apology in the midst of a social exile which regards our discipleship as ridiculous. But walk without fainting we must and we *shall*, just because a worthy walk is promised all who wait for the Lord.

We exiles are sustained in all this just because God's under-standing is unsearchable. God will even use our exile (regardless of the form it takes) in ways we've not yet seen for our edification, our neighbour's encouragement, and for God's own glory.

Then wait for him we shall until that day when faith gives way to sight, exile ended and pilgrimage over, and we are finally, and forever, lost in wonder, love and praise.

Chapter 7

WHEN ONLY AN ANGEL WILL DO

Angels play an indispensable role in our conflicts, and in the ultimate conflict of Christ.

Angels always point us to God and witness to a world that is never ultimately bleak. They surround and sustain us, as they did Jesus, especially during those episodes when our own resources are slender.

They were always an embarrassment when I was a youngster. How could any boy who aspired to be a red-blooded male believe in angels? Besides, what exactly was I supposed to believe in? Ghosts who also happened to be do-gooders? Only hysterical people believed in ghosts, and only silly people had any use for do-gooders!

For most of the year I could remain relatively unembarrassed since angels didn't appear in church-life very often. But Christmas and Easter were especially embarrassing because on these festivals angels were everywhere. In my old age, however, embarrassment has given way to wonder and gratitude. I shouldn't want to be without the angels now.

God's messengers

The Hebrew and Greek words for angel (*malak* and *aggelos*) simply mean "messenger." In some cases what is in a writer's mind is God himself acting as his own messenger. The clue to this use of "angel" is the expression, "the angel of the Lord"; not *"an* angel" or "angels" but *"the* angel of the Lord."

A common pattern emerges as soon as we examine the incident surrounding this expression. Someone wrestles with the angel (like Jacob at the riverbank), or argues with it, flees from it, shouts at it, or trembles before it. Then this person discovers, a day or two later, that she had been contending all along with the living, lordly, sovereign God himself! When she finally grasps that it was *God* she had collided with, her experience of God stamps itself upon her so profoundly that she'll never be able to doubt or deny that it was God. The encounter has rendered her life forever different. "The angel of the Lord" is a Hebrew way of saying "I was seized by the living God himself; I didn't know it at the time, but later I knew it to be God; this awe-ful experience has left me unable to pretend anything else and unable to go back to what I was before the experience." "The angel of the Lord" is God himself acting as his own messenger, stamping himself so startlingly upon someone that this person will bear the impress of his stamp ever after. This person will never confuse the Holy One himself with any God-substitute.

God-substitutes

Let us make no mistake: God-substitutes abound. In ancient Israel one such substitute was the golden calf. The spiritually obtuse knelt down before it. But did they really? No Israelite, however obtuse, pointed to a hunk of metal and said, "That's my god." What he or she worshipped was what the golden calf represented. The metal represented a deity the people could control, one made in their image. No longer did they understand themselves as made in God's image, subject to God's judgement because of the discrepancy between what they had been made and what they had become. A deity made in *their* image was docile, harmless; it could even be manipulated.

The golden calf also represented ethnic advantage. After all, the Hittites had their deity, the Amorites theirs, the Philistines theirs;

each of these ethnic groups claimed their own deity gave them extraordinary advantage. Plainly Israel was not to be left behind. Israel was only too happy to exchange the sovereign ruler of the entire creation for an ethnic booster; at least the latter would give them whatever advantage they needed over their neighbours.

What about us modern types? We say, "He worships his car; she worships her house." But of course he and she do nothing of the sort. She worships what the 4,000-square-foot home represents: social superiority, which is to say, human superiority. He doesn't worship his $80,000 automobile. He worships what it represents. Why, only two generations ago his grandfather had cow-manure on his boots. Today the 32-year old grandson displays his automobile as a monument to his achievement. Just think: a self-made man at 32, for which no one else need be thanked!

When I was a teenager my minister remarked to me, "Imagine, Victor; your grandfather was a bricklayer and your cousin is a urologist!" Is my cousin somehow godlier, holier, better in any sense than my grandfather-bricklayer for possessing expertise at the water-works? In becoming a clergyman have I stalled the Shepherd family's social ascendancy?

We love the gods of our own making. They represent what we give ourselves to and give to ourselves; they reward us with what we have always craved. Only God's own massive assault can shatter these gods. This assault comes often by way of "the angel of the Lord."

Psychology as religion

Professor Paul Vitz teaches psychology at New York University. Several years ago he began to notice that psychology had ceased to be a description of how the human psyche functions; it had elevated itself to the status of religion. Psychology had become a golden calf. People bowed down before it and did obeisance to what it represented. It put itself forward as the final judge of what is true and good; to probe one's psyche was to engage ultimate reality; it had its own high priests, its own sacred vocabulary.

Vitz, still an unbeliever at this point, was disturbed. He didn't know yet precisely or profoundly what it was that was disturbing him. A year or two later, as he came to faith in Jesus Christ (chiefly through reading C.S. Lewis), he knew his disturber had been none other than the angel of the Lord. His life has been different from that point and will be different forever. (Read his book, *Psychology as Religion.*)

One of my friends grew up more or less agnostic. As a teenager he became aware that a cloud of unreality surrounded what most people regarded as substantial. As he came upon item after item of seeming substance riddled with unreality he set it aside. He set more and more aside until he was face-to-face with the one thing that he thought to be more substantial than it even appeared: evil, sheer evil. He couldn't doubt this. Unable to doubt this alone, he found himself living in an unendurable world. (To be convinced only of the presence and pervasiveness of evil is to live in a very bleak world; to be convinced of this as a teenager when all of one's adult life is still in front of oneself is that much worse.)

Finally his languishing gave way to an encounter with the God who has triumphed over evil in his Son. All along, particularly in the bleak days when my friend thought he was contending with nothing more than evil, he was wrestling with the angel of the Lord. He came to see this, know it unshakably, and find himself altered by it forever.

Creatures apart

The more common use of "angel" in scripture, however, refers to someone distinct from God, angels as plural, as special creatures of God. In scripture there are myriads of them. "Heavenly host" is how the description often reads, suggesting innumerable angels. As creatures of pure spirit they do not have bodies of flesh like us. Their function is to witness to God by being servants of God. Because they unfailingly serve God they invariably witness to God.

What are we to make of all this? In view of the heavenly host God's creation is richer than we have always thought. The creation is profoundly, pervasively and finally spiritual.

Most people think not. They insist that matter alone is real. To be sure, Christians would never deny that the material is actual. Trees and mountains, buildings and bridges are not imaginary. Nonetheless, they'd also insist there's a spiritual dimension to the creation much deeper than trees and mountains.

Some would argue that the realm of aesthetics is more real than the material. Mozart's music, Robert Frost's poetry, Tom Thomson's painting, Veronica Tennent's dancing — all of this is oceans deeper than sticks and stones, yet it is not deep enough. Everywhere in creation the really deep things are not finally aesthetic but spiritual.

Angels surround us

Since this is the case, everything we deal with every day has profound spiritual significance just because the heavenly host, the angels, surround everything at all times. Consider the matter of hospitality. The writer of the epistle to the Hebrews states, "Do not neglect to show hospitality to strangers, for thereby some have entertained angels unawares." With our shallower understanding we tend to think that hospitality — feeding someone in our home on Saturday evening — is to meet a physical need (for food), a social need (for company), as well as a psychological need (for interchange with other minds). But if the universe is pervasively spiritual, as the notion of angels attests, then hospitality is fraught with spiritual significance. It is an act that unfolds before God, involving people whom God longs to know and bless as they in turn know him. Therefore our hospitality has sacramental significance; it is used of God in ways not known to us as God secretly infiltrates the lives of those who sit at our dinner table. The mystery of God's secret infiltration is something we cannot control, measure, or even see immediately. But according to the apostles, hospitality is the occasion of God's secret infiltration as few other things are.

Conflict

Think about conflict. Marxists maintain that human conflict, at bottom, is the result of economic forces as the "haves" and the "have-nots" wage war. I should never want to deny the economic dimension to human conflict. To the psychoanalyst human conflict is the result of primal intrapsychic drives that render our unconscious minds a battleground. I should never want to deny this psychoanalytic dimension. To the existentialist philosopher human conflict is the collision of competing wills as each person's will is a will-to-power, a will-to-domination. I should never want to deny this dimension to human conflict.

All of these approaches have a measure of truth and therefore a measure of depth. Yet none goes deep enough; none is ultimately true. Human conflict, ultimately, is a spiritual problem, including the conflict with, and within, one's self.

Jesus was sustained by angels on two occasions of terrible conflict: when he was tried in the wilderness and when he was abandoned in Gethsemane. Conflict raged within him on these occasions — a conflict not economic, psychoanalytic or philosophical, but nakedly spiritual. In the wilderness he was tempted to undermine the kingdom of God, to act on the seduction that there was a shortcut to the kingdom of God when in fact there was none. What was at stake in his temptations? The salvation of every last one of us. Had he succumbed, you and I should be lost eternally.

His temptation to avoid the cross and the dereliction was temptation to second-guess his Father (outright unbelief). It was temptation to secure first and last his own comfort and ease (outright disobedience). It was temptation to forsake us, the very people he has said he came for (outright betrayal).

In Gethsemane his disciples slept because they thought nothing was going on, when in fact spiritual conflict was raging. It raged so fiercely that our Lord needed additional resources, unusual assistance, to survive it — as he did in the wilderness three years earlier. When the gospel-writers tell us he was assisted by angels they're saying his conflict was ultimately spiritual and unimaginably intense. If you and I think our conflicts are anything other or anything less we are shallow.

Thy kingdom come

The kingdom of God occurs wherever God's will is done perfectly. We say in the Lord's Prayer, "Thy kingdom come, thy will be done on earth as it is in heaven." God's will is done, done perfectly, in heaven right now. Scripture speaks of the heavenly host which bears witness to God's kingdom. God has innumerable witnesses in heaven before he has so much as one witness on earth. The kingdom of God has come to earth, we know, in the person of Jesus Christ, for in him God's will is done perfectly. The kingdom he brings with him is witnessed to by the myriad of angels. This means God will always have innumerable witnesses on earth even if earth-born witnesses like you and me are sadly lacking in quality and quantity.

I find immense comfort in what scripture says about angels. However much I may fail my Lord in serving and attesting that kingdom he brings with him, there are other creatures whose service and witness never fail. Therefore the kingdom of God will eventually superimpose itself upon and subdue the kingdoms of this world.

Listen to Karl Barth, the pre-eminent theologian of our century, a thinker of the same stature as Athanasius, Augustine, Anselm, Aquinas, Luther and Calvin. Barth wrote, a few years after World War II, "Because of the angelic witness to God's kingdom we can never find intolerable or hopeless the apparently or genuinely troubled state of things on earth." Just before war had broken out Barth had been apprehended at his Saturday morning lecture in the University of Bonn, Germany. He had been deported immediately from Germany to his native Switzerland. As soon as hostilities with Germany had ceased the cold war with the Soviet Union had begun. While there was no war, hot or cold, in Switzerland, Barth never pretended the Swiss were uncommonly virtuous; he readily admitted his own country funded itself by harbouring the ill-gotten gains (the infamous unnamed accounts in the Swiss banks) of the most despicable criminals throughout the world. Nevertheless, "because of the angelic witness to God's kingdom we can never find intolerable or hopeless the . . . troubled state of things on earth."

Christmas and Easter

The most obvious, angel-saturated developments in the New Testament, of course, are Christmas and Easter. The incarnation is God's incursion of that world he loves profligately even as it resists him defiantly. To see how much it resists him we need only look at Herod, who will go to murderous lengths to undo the beachhead God established as he invaded his world in his Son in order to reclaim it. So intense is the resistance that all of heaven's resources must be mobilized to secure the beachhead and bear witness to it.

At the resurrection of our Lord the angelic hosts appeared again to herald throughout the cosmos the victory God won in raising his Son triumphant over the powers of death. In view of all this Barth's declaration rings and reverberates: *"Because of the angelic witness to God's kingdom we can never find intolerable or hopeless the apparently or genuinely troubled state of things on earth."*

The quintessential human act

What can this knowledge of angels teach us? Because the heavenly host reminds us that everything in life is pervasively spiritual, finally spiritual, the single most important thing any of us can do is pray. Because we are dealing with the spiritual whenever we deal with any aspect or dimension of life, the quintessential human act is prayer.

Further, because the angels bear witness to God, always pointing away from themselves to him whom they serve, the most angelic character the world has seen is John the Baptist. John lived only to point away from himself to Jesus Christ. John neither wanted nor expected an honourary degree, civic reception or special fuss made of him. He was content to say, "He must increase and I must decrease."

Moreover, because the angels magnify the glory of God on earth, therefore the world and human history are never *ultimately* bleak. Evil-ridden, yes; pain-ridden, yes; incapable of saving itself, yes. Nevertheless because "our great God and Saviour" cherishes his creation, and because the angels magnify God's glory on earth in the midst of our history, our situation is never finally bleak. Like the angels, one day we too shall see God's glory everywhere when the kingdom of God, hidden now, is made manifest to all.

When next you come upon the word "angel" know that either it refers to "the angel of the Lord," God himself acting as his own messenger, *or* to that spirit-creature whose witness to God is unambiguous just because its service of God is unrelenting.

Then you must think of the heavenly host, myriads of angels that surround us especially during those episodes when our own resources are slender and only the resources of him who sustained his Son will do for us. Wherever we struggle in life, our struggle is finally spiritual, and will be until that day when the earth is no longer troubled and the kingdom of God has eclipsed the kingdoms of this world.

WINTER

Pain in the Wilderness

Grace is ours even in winter. Snowed in and chilled by adversity and isolation, our enforced "hibernation" will find us gathering strength for re-emergence later.

Chapter 8

JETTISONING FEAR IN HARD TIMES

We must look not to the weakness of our faith but to the strength of Jesus

Fear is easy in hard times. Yet Jesus' most frequent command is "Fear not!" The solution is to fill our minds and hearts with the promises of the God who knows every detail of our lives.

There are days when our faith seems so strong we couldn't imagine it stronger. The sun is shining on us, our children are healthy, our job is rewarding, no one is after us, and a good and gracious God is running the universe. Only the blind or ungrateful would feel differently. Lack of faith, it seems to us on such days, is not so much a spiritual problem as an intellectual deficiency.

Then there are days when we have to struggle for faith. A friend of mine was diagnosed with, and treated for, oral cancer. Recently his wife of 25 years left him for another man. More recently he was dismissed from his job. Worse, the committee that dismissed him suggested moral taint surrounded him yet refused to say what the taint was or how they heard of it. Faith became a struggle.

We can all resonate with the frantic father of Mark 9 who pleaded with Jesus, "I do believe, but can't you do something about the *un*faith that threatens to drag my faith under and drown it?"

Even in our best days, our faith is never so strong that it doesn't need strengthening, never so unmixed with unfaith that it doesn't need fortifying.

We realize how much we need to keep our faith strong and our outlook positive *as soon as hard times come upon us.* These can take many forms.

One is personal adversity. However much we all want to render permanent the good time we're having now, we know we can't. The wheel of fortune turns, and yesterday's "end of a perfect day" is not guaranteed for tomorrow. Not only do circumstances change, they change unforeseeably. Developments we never even imagined materialize before us and we've neither time to prepare ourselves for them nor tried-and-true tools for handling them.

Hard times can also include what I call "intra-psychic baggage." Some people have besetting mental/emotional afflictions rooted in body-chemistry imbalances. These people will have to take medicine all their lives. Even so, the drug doesn't alleviate their distress entirely; they suffer more than most of us are aware.

Then there are those whose besetting mental/emotional afflictions are rooted in emotional injuries. Childhood wounds have scarred them profoundly; in adult life the wounds continue to haunt them, even warp them. A young woman undergoing psychotherapy told me that by the time she was 30 years old she had lived in 44 different homes. Her parents, burdened with their own intra-psychic baggage, "coped" with life by fleeing. When this woman was a teenager her father, to whom she related very ambivalently, was killed in an industrial accident.

The "hard times" that expose faith's frailty may be our awareness of hard times elsewhere in the world — the shocking unfairness of it all. Many people's belief in God is relatively cozy until they learn not only of the genocide in Europe during the 1940s, but of the "killing fields" of Cambodia during the '70s, the slaughter of the Iraqis during the '80s and of the Sinhalese during the '90s. "Does it ever end?" they ask. Once they realize *it's the way human history unfolds*, cozy belief turns into a desperate struggle for faith — or it gives up and doesn't struggle at all.

Where faith is difficult, fear is easy. Everywhere in scripture the antithesis of faith is fear, not doubt. "Fear not" is the most frequent command on the lips of Jesus just because fear routs faith. To have faith *is* to fear not.

Nevertheless we do fear. The company we work for has merged with a larger one and not all personnel will be retained. Our child seems unwell and we've just just enough medical knowledge not to be put off by our friends' reassurances that there's nothing wrong. We're afraid that the psychological booby-trap we've hidden or disguised for years; that situation where we appear helpless, weak and silly, is going to become publicly evident and we shall be humiliated. We're afraid that since we're not yet married we're never to be married. (I also meet people who fear they'll never get *un*married.) Then there is a different kind of fear, unattached to any specific object or occurrence: "existential anxiety," mental health experts call it, that niggling, semi-conscious awareness of our fragility and ultimate impotence in the face of life's accidentality and our own mortality.

Even though "Fear not!" echoes throughout the gospels, we feel it has as much effect as our going down to Lake Ontario and telling the waves to stop rolling in.

How can we learn to jettison our fear in hard times?

The promises of God

We must fill up our mind and heart with the promises of God. They're what I sought to have my daughters memorize when they were younger. "The day may come," I said in my most fatherly wisdom, "when your life has capsized and you won't be able to read or reason or do much else. In that day you'll be able only to mumble over and over what has gone so deep into your head that it will bubble up within you for as long as you're breathing." And so we set about learning such promises as

Fear not, for I have redeemed you; I have called you by name, you are mine. When you pass through the waters I will be with you; and through the rivers, they shall not overwhelm you.

When you walk through the fire you shall not be burned,
and the flame shall not consume you. For I am the Lord your
God, the Holy One of Israel, your Saviour (Isaiah 43:1-3).

John Newton is known to many through his hymn, "Amazing
Grace." The startling about-face in his life — from vulgar sailor
and slave-ship captain to Anglican clergyman and hymnwriter —
made him sensational. But his little book, *Letters of Christian
Counsel*, has shown him to be profound. There he points out that
the promises of God have immediate reference to "hard times."
While we may believe them with our head at any time, it's only in
hard times that we *prove* them. Did Newton himself prove them?
On the Sunday morning following the most difficult day of his life
— the day his wife was buried, he and she having loved each other
since their teenage years — Newton staggered into his pulpit and
preached from the Book of the prophet Habakkuk.

Though the fig tree do not blossom, nor fruit be on the vines,
the produce of the olive fail and the fields yield no food,
the flock be cut off from the fold and there be no herd in the
stalls,
*Yet I will rejoice in the Lord, I will joy in the God of my
salvation.*
God, the Lord, is my strength.

He affirmed it, repeated it, leaned on it, even if he never felt
worse in his life.

God counts hairs

Many bad jokes have been made of our Lord's insistence that even
the hairs of our head are numbered. By this he meant we're of such
value to God that no detail of our life escapes him. I had a glimmer
of this as I learned afresh how one human being can be inestimably
dear to another. As Oliver Sacks worked in a state hospital in New
York, each day brought before him men and women afflicted with
tics, small, jerky, convulsive movements. In one particular woman

he counted 300 different tics. As I read his account of her medical problems it was obvious Sacks didn't add them up in order to satisfy clinical curiosity or to write a research article for a prestigious medical journal. He simply cared for a suffering person, and cared overwhelmingly. If a woman so badly afflicted that the rest of the world writes her off as discardable means this much to Oliver Sacks, what do people like you and me, undergoing hard times, mean to God?

Sacks counts tics; God counts hairs. In both cases someone is dear to someone else. Still, at the end of the day Sacks could not relieve the woman; he could love her, but he could not finally alleviate her affliction.

It is different with God. He not only cares so much, he cares so effectively that at the end of our journey he will have preserved us against every kind of dissolution and caused us to stand before him uncrumbled, undisintegrated, whole.

Plainly, Sacks knew his patients exceedingly well. Yet God's knowledge of us is much more than mere detailed information about our lives. When scripture repeatedly says *God knows us* it means he has bound himself firmly to us and us to him. God has us so deep and fast in his love and purpose that he will unfailingly accomplish in us precisely what he has in mind for us.

Think of a woodworker turning a crude block of wood on his lathe. He picks up one chisel after another, occasionally adjusting the speed of the lathe. Bystanders try to guess what the outcome is going to be: a table-leg? a desk-lamp? a banister-post? With a subtle smile the woodworker says to the guessers, "You're all wrong; I know what it's going to be." It's not merely that he has information they lack; it's rather that he, the knower, is the maker, and to know what the finished product is going to be is to be fashioning it all the time.

When God called Jeremiah to be a prophet he said, "Before I formed you in the womb I knew you . . . I appointed you to be a prophet to the nations." God's purpose for Jeremiah was to speak the truth of God to the rulers of the nations. In knowing him God unfailingly fulfills his purpose for him. When God knows you and me he unfailingly fulfills his purpose for us. No disaster, betrayal, affliction or attrition will ever deflect or defeat him.

It's not God's purpose that we all be prophets like Jeremiah. But he does intend that we be restored wholly, the nicks and tics of our bodies, minds and spirits eliminated finally. We shall then be perfectly restored to that image in which he created us so as to reflect his glory.

Jesus says, "I know my sheep . . . I give them eternal life . . . no one shall snatch them out of my hand." Consider the logic of our Lord's pronouncement. Because he knows us, nothing can finally impede or frustrate his purpose for us. No affliction or distress can shrivel us until we slip between his fingers, regardless of how we feel.

Scripture speaks both of God's knowledge of us and of our knowledge of God. We must note which is prior and determinative: *God's knowledge of us!* Our security rests not in our grip on him but in his grip on us.

When adversity next howls down upon you and you feel yourself getting fretful over the slenderness of your knowledge of God, remind yourself that God knows you perfectly *now*; therefore nothing can separate you from his love in Christ Jesus.

That was another promise I had my daughters memorize. I told them this verse was not only the climax of Romans 8 and of the Roman epistle, but the climax of *all of scripture*: "Neither death nor life, neither cosmic forces nor earthly institutions, neither present developments nor past disasters nor future horrors, *nothing* can separate us from the love of God in Christ Jesus our Lord."

Once this promise is tattooed onto our hearts and engraved into our brains we find other promises lighting up for us. Psalm 27: "The Lord is my light and my salvation, whom shall I fear? The Lord is the stronghold of my life, of whom shall I be afraid?" No wonder the psalmist can sum it all up in five words of one syllable each: *"He will keep your life"* (Psalm 121).

Any distraction will do

When people undergo very hard times and want to know how faith can be "kept," they often tell me they feel guilty for having such weak faith. (Feeling guilty for weak faith, I might add, never yet made anyone's faith stronger.) Next they tell me they will have to pray more, with greater ardour, at greater length. But in their heart of hearts they know what all of us have learned when life capsizes: they can't pray. Therefore I never urge people whose faith has been hammered by adversity to pray more. This will only make them feel weaker and magnify their self-rejection.

I tell them not to be concerned about praying. Here I borrow from the wisdom of Ecclesiastes: "For everything there is a season, and a time for every matter under heaven." I'm convinced there is a time to pray and a time to be distracted.

Distraction is marvellously effective. Think of people who are undergoing terrific temptation. In their last-ditch effort at resisting it they ask me if they shouldn't pray more for strength to resist. "No!" I tell them. "As long as you're praying about your temptation you're keeping it in the forefront of your mind, feeding it, its grip on you growing by the minute. Don't pray about it; go to a ball game!" Any distraction will do! Distraction will not overturn the adversity that has bombed us; but it will get it out of the forefront of our minds. Wise spiritual counsellors know when to counsel prayer and when to counsel distraction.

Plainly we cannot distract ourselves. Our friends must help us. They must put an arm around us and carry us off somewhere with them, even if only for a while, lest our burden become yet more burdensome. I think often of the four men who brought their paralysed friend to Jesus. The text says, "When Jesus saw their faith . . ." Whose faith? Throughout the passage "they" refers to *the four men only*. They brought their friend to Jesus and at the Master's word he was restored.

On several occasions in my life a few people have had to do as much for me — as I have had to for them. Our friends are simply indispensable when adversity has laid us low and we can't feel or find any faith within us. At such a time our friends will believe the promises for us, and continue to believe them until we've recovered enough to affirm them again for ourselves.

Looking unto Jesus

We need a positive outlook, yet a realistic one. Some people say, "Don't look back; you'll be undone as you recall the negativities that haunt the past." Others say, "Don't look ahead; you'll be immobilized by the whirlpools that await you." Then where do we look?

The writer of Hebrews says it best: "Keep on looking unto Jesus, the pioneer and perfecter of our faith." As long as we look to Jesus it's safe to look back, for then we see his victory in being raised from the dead — a victory that can never be overturned. Only then it is safe to look ahead, for we foresee the public manifestation of his victory. Looking unto Jesus — seeing both past and future through him — is the one thing that *will* strengthen our faith.

Our faith will never increase as long as we keep looking at our own faith. (In fact, the more we look at it the weaker it will appear.) Faith grows as we look to him who is the author and object of whatever faith we have, Jesus Christ our Lord. With such a positive outlook we shall run with perseverance the race that is set before us, knowing that nothing can separate us from the love of God in him who ran the race ahead of us, who endured hard times, who is our victorious companion on the way, and who will see us home at last.

Chapter 9

WHO ARE THE POOR?

Hard times often spiral down into poverty:
spiritual and social as well as material.

Who are the poor?
What does it mean to
"remember" them? Far
from a romantic notion
providing fodder for the
righteous, the poor are
any in extreme need
of any sort. The
unshrunken heart must
throb with the suffering
of a fellow-sufferer.

Who are the poor? Those who lack money? In 1968 I was an impecunious student at the University of Toronto. But even though I lacked money, was I poor? That year I was hospitalized for 45 consecutive days. I was seen daily by the physician who admitted me, as well as by the orthopedic surgeon who had me placed in a body-cast. When I was discharged from hospital the orthopedist continued to see me until he deemed me fit to play hockey again. I had received medical treatment incomparably better than the treatment 99 percent of the world will ever see; I was treated at a hospital whose services cost hundreds of dollars per bed per day. At the end of it all my expenses were zero.

When in 1986 my mother was hospitalized for 75 consecutive days, she too was billed nothing. Since she is over 65 she pays nothing directly for her medication. Could she ever be poor?

Recently I took the several cases of apple juice my wife had purchased to Foodpath, Mississauga's well-known foodbank. When I arrived I found many clients waiting to have a food-hamper filled. None of them appeared rich. But in view of the fact that they'd never be allowed to go hungry, how poor were they when compared to the 35,000 people who starve to death every day?

If to be poor is to be without food, clothing, elemental education and medical care, then it would appear difficult to be poor in Canada.

Material misery

Yet even in Canada there are those whose material misery (to speak of only one kind of misery) is so very pronounced that we do not hesitate to call them poor, regardless of the definition of poverty. Think of the 25,000 "double-bunked" people in Toronto. One family, adults and children, rents a two-bedroom apartment-unit. The entire family sleeps in one bedroom. This family in turn sub-lets its second bedroom to another family. Now we have eight or nine people living in a two-bedroom apartment, elbowing each other aside to get into kitchen and washroom. Can you imagine the frustration, the flare-ups, born of overcrowding? Is it any wonder that from time-to-time someone "boils over" and the police are called to yet another domestic irruption? What school-performance can be expected of children in such a setting? Two television sets blaring, no defensible space, no solitude, no incentive to study. A further and frightening dimension to this state of affairs is that since education is the single most effective means of escaping poverty, lack of educational opportunity and encouragement fixes yet another generation in the same sort of poverty.

When I was living undercover in Parkdale while researching a magazine article on chronically mentally ill people I learned that the more severe one's illness (itself a form of poverty, intellectual and emotional), the worse one's living accommodation. I visited several of the area's infamous boarding houses. The worst one was indescribable: it housed two dozen people who were utterly deranged. Never mind that social assistance pays their rent and thus forestalls death by exposure; never mind that when they have appendicitis they can get a free appendectomy; they are deranged, live in degrading filth, and someone's throwing eversomuch more money at them would still find them poor in any non-economic sense of the term.

When I was newly-ordained Maureen and I found ourselves in a small village of northeastern New Brunswick. Most families there were sustained by fishing or lumberjacking or peat-bog excavating. The villages surrounding ours were sustained in the same way yet were manifestly wretched! Shanty-houses with earth floors; two-by-four partitions but no walls. All of us have seen icicles hanging from the outside of a home; have you ever seen them hanging from the inside? Why was it that our community and the neighbouring ones fished the same water and cut the same trees, yet our village appeared relatively resplendent?

When we moved east we had just finished reading Catherine Marshall's novel, *Christie*, with its heart-catching character, Fairlie. The first time Maureen met Opal Murray she rushed home and shouted, "I've just met Fairlie, right out of the book!" A few days later Opal, together with a friend, called on Maureen and announced, "We's here to learn you about babies." (The learning "took," I might add.) Opal and her husband Jack lived in a home that had been a fish-processing plant. They had purchased it for a few dollars, the only few dollars they had. As a result their six children had slept on straw ticks. Come Sunday morning all eight of them appeared at church radiant, happy, confident. Opal said she couldn't afford shampoo and so she washed her children's heads (in rural New Brunswick you don't wash your hair, you wash your head) with a bar of Sunlight soap. When Maureen had to be hospitalized for surgery Opal and Jack had me to their home for supper. As Opal served up thick slices of bologna Jack beamed at me and said, without a hint of embarrassment but with more than a hint of triumph, "Victor, it's poor man's steak!" And so we feasted.

Were Jack and Opal poor?

To lack recognition

Anyone is poor who lacks recognition. When Elie Wiesel was a

15-year-old in Auschwitz an S.S. guard taunted him, "I know why you want to survive, young man; you want to tell the world how horrific Auschwitz and its perpetrators were. But the world will never believe you. So horrific is this camp that no one will believe your testimony, and you will have survived for naught."

On the other hand to be recognized is always to be non-poor, whether one has much money or little. Ned Vladomansky was a Czechoslovakian hockey player whom Harold Ballard wanted for the Leafs. Because he was recognized his escape from Czechoslovakia was engineered and his flight to Canada paid for even as Canadian immigration officials lied through their teeth and falsified every document they laid their hands on, as ordered by their political superiors. Never mind that Vladomansky was a dud as an N.H.L. player and therefore didn't draw a rich man's salary. He was recognized. People in Ireland have waited 25 years to emigrate to Canada. But they aren't recognized. They are poor.

Who are the poor? We must each answer the question for ourselves. It can mean those who lack money or health, friends, opportunity, responsible parents or support.

Remembering the poor

The apostle Paul tells the church in Galatia he is "eager to remember the poor." He insists all Christians remember the poor. The Hebrew meaning of "remember" doesn't mean to recall an idea or a concept; it's to make something outside ourselves in space and time a living actuality within ourselves right now. At the last supper, when Jesus took bread and wine and said, "Do this in remembrance of me," he didn't mean we're to recall the idea or notion of his sacrifice. He meant that his sacrifice, an event outside us in space and time and which forms the pattern or template of our discipleship, is to become a living actuality within us — now and always. As we "remember" his sacrifice we find our sin borne and borne away, live in the freedom that is now ours, and cheerfully walk the road of crossbearing discipleship ourselves. That which is outside us is to become a living actuality within us so that our heartbeat and the heartbeat of the poor are one. We have identified ourselves so thoroughly with the poor that they now have the freedom and the desire to identify themselves with us.

The poor, to us, can only be identified by us. It could be someone without money or dental plan who needs dental work done. It could just as easily be the richest person in town whose loneliness or anxiety are off the chart. It could be the youngster whose appearance or manner or ethnicity finds him picked on. It could be the deranged person who has been robbed again as schizophrenics are easy to rob and hurt. Once we have decided "who are the poor," we must be sure to "remember" them.

The romantics among us like to romanticize poverty. But there is nothing at all romantic about poverty, as the poor have always known. Such romantics wrongly assume there is something righteous about poverty. If poverty were inherently righteous it would be our responsibility to increase the world's poverty, thereby increasing the world's righteousness. On the contrary, scripture insists that poverty is evil; like any evil it must be resisted and repulsed, even eradicated.

Wasn't Jesus poor himself? one might ask. It all depends on what we mean by "poor." He wasn't financially poor. During the years of his public ministry he was never gainfully employed. Anyone who can thrive without being gainfully employed is not poor financially. Jesus (and the twelve) were funded by wealthy women (Luke 8:3). He never hesitated to accept their support, to eat and drink the sumptuous fare the rich offered him — even to the extent that his enemies accused him of "pigging out" and overdoing the wine. When he died soldiers gambled for his cloak, so valuable did they deem it; they didn't toss it aside as worthless. The poor are those in extreme need of any sort. Was our Lord ever in extreme need? We read that he wept, sweat blood, cried out, was so distracted that he stumbled repeatedly.

Poverty is blessed

While poverty is never pronounced righteous, it is pronounced blessed. In Luke's gospel Jesus says, "Blessed are you poor, for yours is the kingdom of God"; in Matthew's gospel, "Blessed are the poor in spirit, for theirs is the kingdom of heaven." "Kingdom of God" and "kingdom of heaven" amount to the same thing.

What's the difference between "poor" and "poor in spirit"? "Blessed are the poor" means "blessed are those in extreme need." "Blessed are the poor in spirit" means "blessed are those who admit their spiritual emptiness, hollowness and inertness." The two expressions don't mean exactly the same thing. Nonetheless those who are in extreme need are more likely to admit spiritual need. Poverty is blessed, says Jesus, not because poverty is good, but because the poor are more likely to cry to God with the hymnwriter, "Nothing in my hand I bring; *nothing!*" They're more likely to see that the consolations of the world are finally spurious.

One of the world's consolations is wealth. Has wealth ever improved the spiritual condition of anyone? It has spelled the spiritual ruin of countless. What does wealth bring finally but a shrunken heart? Another of the world's consolations is adulation. What does adulation bring finally but a swollen head? Poverty isn't blessed because it is good, but because those in extreme need have the fewest pretenses about themselves and their profounder need, even their ultimate need — which, of course, is their need of the saving God. The more extreme our need, the less likely we are to think we need nothing, that we don't even need the One who claims us for himself by his generosity in creation and claims us for himself again by his mercy in redemption.

What can we do?

When we come upon extreme need of any sort what can we do? What step do we take to "remember" the poor? I don't think we can specify this in advance; there's no formula or magic recipe. There is only our Spirit-sensitized discernment of poverty of any sort; there is only the unshrunken heart that throbs with the suffering of a fellow-sufferer; the unswollen head that apprehends the specific cross a specific disciple is to shoulder in view of someone else's specific need.

One thing we must never do is use the text, "The poor you have with you always" (Mark 14:9), as a pretext for doing nothing. A grateful woman lavishes the costliest perfume — 20 ounces of "Escape" — on our Lord. Some hard-hearted nit-pickers pick, "It could have been sold and the proceeds given to the poor." Yes, it could have. But life can't be reduced to the functional. Unselfconscious gratitude can't be measured. Love can't be exchanged for currency. The kingdom of God, while certainly including the material, cannot be reduced to the material. The woman's gratitude was incalculable just because her spiritual need had been bottomless and our Lord's gift of himself to her unfathomable. Those who object to what she has done are not yet poor in spirit themselves. Would to God they were simply poor, for if they were they might also be poor in spirit and then would find themselves made rich by the only Saviour they can ever have.

While not everyone is poor in the sense of extreme financial, social, or emotional need, every last person *is* poor in the sense of extreme spiritual need. Since this is the case, we shall always be safe in beginning here as we endeavour to remember the poor.

I am moved every time I read the Book of Jonah. Jonah failed to grasp the enormity of the spiritual need of the Ninevites. Finally God jerked Jonah awake and told him of his immense pity for a vast city whose people did not know their right hand from their left. Centuries later Jesus would look out on crowds and say to his disciples, "See? Sheep without a shepherd!" But our Lord did more than say the crowd knew not right hand from left. The Greek text tells us that at the sight of the crowd his gut knotted and pain pierced him as though he had been stabbed.

If we begin with the assumption of spiritual poverty, we shall soon find ourselves drawn into the orbit of those whose need of the Good Shepherd is extreme. Once in their orbit we shall find their needs, like ours, to be many and manifold, *and manifest.* At this point we shall never have to ask, "But what are we to do? How are the poor to be 'remembered'?" We shall *know.* And the poor will know as well.

Chapter 10

SIGNIFICANCE IN OUR SUFFERING

As we joyfully offer them up to God as sacrifices, our afflictions cease to be unrelieved negativities.

To take up with Christ is to take up our cross. Affliction and persecution are badges of honour. But "Be of good cheer," Jesus says. Our crosses can actually become instruments of life and healing to others.

A beach holiday looks good in the March break. Snow-shovelling is behind us, heating-bills are decreasing, and the cough-syrup stays in the bottle. When the travel company dangles warmer climes in front of us, few things ever looked so good!

There is a kind of preaching that is just like this. People are jaded on account of life's jostlings. The preacher speaks of joy, peace and contentment; great surges of strength and wonderful infusions of enthusiasm. The preacher links it all to Jesus. When he dangles Jesus in front of jaded people, it's all as attractive as the prospect of a beach holiday in the March break.

There's only one problem with the preacher's presentation, but it's a big one: regardless of what he says, in fact *he has left out Jesus.* He *thinks* he has included him, since he ascribes all the "goodies" we get to him. But the huge error the preacher has made is this: he thinks we can have all that our Lord genuinely wants to give us *without having our Lord himself.* But we can't.

Jesus Christ does not give us joy, peace, contentment, strength and enthusiasm as though he were dispensing tonic from a medicine bottle. Our Lord can only give us himself. In so doing he gives us "all things with him," in the words of Paul. Popular preachers today persist in overlooking something crucial: to be bound to Jesus Christ is *to be bound to a cross.* Jesus warmly invited people to become disciples. But he also told them there was no discipleship, no intimacy with him, apart from cross-bearing.

This is not to deny that fellowship with Jesus Christ is glorious. He brings us a peace the world cannot bring, a peace "that passes all understanding." At the same time, fellowship with our Lord is double-sided: he insisted he brings not peace but a sword, wielded by a hostile world which stabs and slashes his disciples.

When the mother of James and John asked Jesus if her two sons could have extraordinary places of honour in the kingdom of God, Jesus, as was his custom, answered with a question of his own: "Can your two sons withstand getting kicked in the teeth on account of me?"

Cross-bearing is as essential to discipleship as are obedience, prayer or worship. We don't become disciples and then discover, much later, that every now and then there's a minor down-side to it all. Quite the contrary. Jesus calls us saying, "I promise you such blessing as to be available nowhere else, so wonderful that you may describe it but never explain it. But I also promise you suffering you have never imagined. Now do you still want me?"

Count it all joy

The New Testament never moves away from this conviction. In the Sermon on the Mount Jesus says, "Blessed are those who are persecuted for righteousness' sake." Elsewhere he says, "you cannot be my disciple unless you take up your cross." In Acts 5 the apostles finally leave the Sanhedrin (the church courts) "rejoicing that they were counted worthy to suffer dishonour for [Christ's] name." Paul writes matter-of-factly, "Anyone who desires to live a godly life in Christ Jesus will be persecuted." James encourages his readers,

"Count it all joy . . . when you meet various trials."

To shun cross-bearing — to shun the suffering that comes as a result of faithfulness to our Lord — is to *shun our Lord himself.* Peter wept heart-brokenly in the wake of his denial. Peter had seen that the most intense suffering would shortly be visited upon Jesus. Quickly he disowned any connection with Jesus in order to spare himself similar suffering. In the same instant Peter knew he had divorced himself from the one for whom he had earlier said he would walk on broken glass.

Christians live in the world. Yet many are surprisingly naive about the simple fact that the world is hostile to Jesus Christ and therefore to the gospel. The world, however, is *not* hostile to religion. It tolerates it, approves it, considers it a mark of sophistication and broad-mindedness. As long as Christian discipleship, so-called, passes itself off as religion, all is well. But as soon as Jesus Christ is seen to contradict or condemn the world's self-understanding and self-projection, Christ's people are set upon.

When Jesus sent out his missioners he said, "I am sending you out as sheep in the midst of wolves; you're going to get flogged in the churches." (Why would the church flog apostles of Jesus? Because religion is acceptable in the church as it is in the world; whereas Jesus Christ, his truth and his people are not.) "You will be hounded by all on account of me," the Master said chillingly. In John's gospel Jesus earnestly prayed for his people: "Father, "I have given them your word; and the world has hated them because they are not of the world, even as I am not of the world."

Disturbers of the peace

But why does the world (including a worldly church) hate our Lord and his people? Because it sees Christians as disturbers of the peace. Jesus himself is a great disturber. He and the world collide. Righteousness and sin cannot be reconciled. Truth exposes falsehood for what it is. Transparency shames duplicity. The kingdom of God and the work of the evil one are forever incompatible.

The irony of it all, of course, is that Jesus is the world's friend as no one else is; yet the world hates the only one who can save it.

Christians stand with their Lord in solidarity with the world for the sake of the world; yet the world abuses them.

There is no escape: to be a Christian is always to be saddled with hostility.

Phases of affliction

Affliction at the hands of the world often progresses through three phases. First, defamation. Accusations are made that are simply not true. Second, ostracism. You aren't on the inner circle any longer (if you ever were). Third, out-and-out abuse. Jesus himself illustrates this progression. He was called a demon-possessed bastard, relegated to the fringes of the religious establishment, then finally "terminated."

What have you been called? In the course of the resistance movement and struggle within my denomination I've heard things said of me that are simply not true. It used to bother me terribly, but now it doesn't at all. I've learned to view it as a badge of honour, a mark of discipleship.

"Cross-bearing" defined

When people speak of bearing their crosses, however, they customarily mean not that extraordinary suffering brought upon us through our loyalty to him whom the world rejects; they mean that ordinary suffering that comes to us simply because we're fragile creatures who live in an unpredictable environment. We fall sick, our teenager gets derailed, our aged parent is chronically confused, our brother-in-law is as mean as a junk-yard dog, we lose our job. We sigh with genuine weariness and wonder how we are going to "bear our cross."

Such suffering, however, is never referred to in scripture as a cross to be borne. If tomorrow I am found to have encephalitis or Lou Gehrig's disease it will be dreadful, but it's not a "cross." It is suffering brought on me simply through being human, not through being a disciple.

We can learn much here from our Roman Catholic fellow-believers. They acknowledge that the ordinary suffering we incur simply through being human, *if borne cheerfully, without bitterness, rancour or resentment,* can become a sacrifice offered up to God. Thus it obtains a similar significance to that of suffering incurred through being a disciple.

It comes naturally to us to resent suffering, to chafe under it, be embittered by it and then poison ever so many others on account of it. Left to ourselves this is how we fallen human beings react. It is by grace, by our "looking unto Jesus," that the suffering we neither brought on ourselves nor are able to get rid of *doesn't* embitter and disfigure us.

If, as our Roman Catholic friends insist, suffering borne in this way is indeed a sacrifice offered up to God, then it is legitimate for us to speak of it as a cross to be borne. After all, it is our discipleship that keeps us looking unto Jesus in the midst of our ineradicable suffering.

Some years ago I was a speaker at a summer conference during which there was a healing service where the worship-leader laid hands upon people as he prayed for them. Two people at this event captured my attention: a 60-year-old woman, a widow, together with her 35-year old son. The woman, a Registered Nurse, had undergone a small stroke that inhibited movement in one arm and one leg. She hobbled. Her son, on the other hand, was very ill. Severely schizophrenic, he lived with his mother. She struggled to go to work every day despite her disabilities, even as she had to look after her ill son. In the afternoon before the evening's healing service the son and I were sitting in front of the coffee machine chatting about anything at all. Suddenly he faced me in dead earnestness and said, "At the service tonight I am coming to you in order to have you lay hands on me. I want to be free from the voices; you know, the voices." My heart sank. I staggered to my feet, bought us each an ice-cream cone, and took him for a walk.

Ever since then I have pondered his unrelieved suffering, his mother's difficulty, the struggle she has day by day — *and the genuine cheerfulness in which she contends with it all.* That's what I ponder most: her transparent good nature and cheerfulness in the face of life's challenges. By her looking unto Jesus, her suffering which isn't a consequence of her discipleship is profoundly transmuted before God. By looking unto Jesus she has offered up to him what would otherwise embitter and disfigure her even as it has poisoned others in similar situations.

No complaints

While passage after passage in the New Testament insists that cross-bearing is a necessary part of discipleship, in no passage does it speak of this in terms of protest or complaint. No bewailing our fate, griping or self-pity. Why not? Because Christians of apostolic discernment and experience know that Christ's cross is that by which he conquers. His resurrection means not that his cross has been left behind but that his cross continues to be effective. His resurrection is precisely what makes his *ongoing* suffering victorious in the world.

Few people understand that the risen Jesus suffers still. Many assume Jesus had a bad day one Friday, then a super day on Easter Sunday and things have gone swimmingly ever since. They assume in his resurrection Jesus left his crucifiedness behind him forever.

Not so! It was the risen Christ who said to Thomas, "Look at my gaping wounds!" Even raised he is still wounded! It was the risen Christ who cried out to Paul, "Why are you persecuting me?" when Paul (then Saul) was persecuting Christ's people. The risen one suffers still! However, his resurrection means his ongoing suffering is now the leading edge of God's victory in the world.

The cross you and I bear is the leading edge of God's victory over whatever evil laps at our lives. Taken up into this victory ourselves, we know the afflictions we bear will never best us. Indeed, our affliction itself will be used of God to alleviate someone else's affliction. Is it not Christ's wounds that heal us? His death that brings us life? His suffering that comforts us? Then as cross-bearers with him it is our privilege to be used of him in similar manner on behalf of many others.

None of this is to suggest cross-bearing is pleasant or ever will be. It is difficult, and frequently dreadful. Our Lord knows this. That's why he urges patience and cheerfulness upon his people: "In the world you will have tribulation, but be of good cheer, the world is precisely what I have overcome" (John 16:33).

However intense our suffering, nevertheless, we're not simply to hang on grimly until the day when we're finally relieved by him who has overcome the world. Christ's people are those who have "tasted the goodness of the word of God and the powers of the age to come." What we have already tasted convinces us that it is real. It quickens our longing for more and assures us that what we've already tasted and now long for God will supply one day in fullest measure.

Paul says that the life of Christ's people, our true life, is at present "hid with Christ in God. When Christ who is our life appears, we shall appear with him in glory" (Colossians 3:3,4). Then may you and I ever be found cheerfully bearing whatever cross we must. For just as our Lord endured suffering and shame only to be vindicated before the entire creation, so shall we be vindicated as his people; for he will have brought us, cross and all, through that turbulent, treacherous world he has overcome on behalf of every one of us.

Chapter 11

ENCOURAGEMENT FOR DEEPSEA FISHERS

When the catch is slim and the prospects grim,
like Peter we must "put out into the deep."

Secularization continues to drain Christian influence in our land. Rather than merely borrow the world's agenda, we must move out to greater depths in obedience to God, holding up the irreducible substance of the gospel with patience and persistence.

Sunday attendance at mainline churches in Canada peaked in 1965. Turn-outs have decreased every year since then. There's no indication the trend is about to change. Our society is vastly more secularized than our foreparents could ever have imagined. An entire generation of young adults now has no "Christian memory"; they were not taken to Sunday School, were never exposed to worship, have grown up without any instruction in elementary Christian truths, and are wholly ignorant of the Bible. Today teachers of English literature must assume their students are unable to recognize the biblical allusions which saturate English literature.

Only a few years ago the hardest-bitten atheist still spoke of being "a good Samaritan." The mother who was alienated from the church still longed for the return of her "prodigal." Even the sportswriter bemoaned the team owner's "crucifixion" of the coach.

In the province of Quebec (whose educational system is still in the hands of a denomination that has never altered its prohibition of birth control) the birthrate went from the highest in Canada to the lowest in only a few years. So much for the church's influence there!

No wonder we shake our heads nostalgically when we read in the gospel that the crowds "pressed upon Jesus to hear the Word of God." The scene (Luke 5) recalls St. James United Church, Montreal, in the 1930s when the preacher was Lloyd C. Douglas. He was writing such bestselling novels as *Magnificent Obsession* and *The Robe*. The sanctuary, which seats 3,600, was full twice a Sunday. Today 35 people gather there for worship.

The process of secularization continues. It appears there is nothing we can do in the face of it.

Yet there is! Like the apostle Peter, spokesperson for all the disciples throughout the gospels, we must "put out into the deep." In obedience to the command of Jesus he moved out to greater depths.

Shallowness attracts no one

In a secular age the church must understand that shallowness attracts no one; it even puts people off. We haven't always been aware of this. For decades we borrowed the world's agenda unthinkingly. We conformed to what we assumed was expected of us, thinking that making ourselves "relevant" would render us effective. When the human potential movement came along (Sensitivity Groups, Transcendental Meditation, Transactional Analysis, even the bizarre notion that preaching is group therapy) we co-opted it uncritically. We assumed the world's wisdom equaled the truth and reality of the kingdom of God. We used a biblical vocabulary without really grasping the force of the words. We recited liturgies while unaware that liturgy is the theatricalization of that Word which is "sharper than a two-edged sword."

In it all we failed to grasp something crucial: the gospel is by nature a counter-cultural movement! The gospel speaks of a *new* creation; therein it contradicts the world's self-understanding. Society doesn't need the church to inform the public of how the public is thinking; it knows this already. Society does need the church, however, to acquaint it with the truth and wisdom, purpose and persistence of the God whose depths are fathomless. In a secular society the church will prove profoundly winsome only as it embodies and exemplifies this very depth itself.

Yet to "go deeper" doesn't mean that the church's credibility and the church's message will be restored immediately. There will be no instant success. It was for good reason Jesus called the first leaders of his church from the ranks of fishermen: those whose everyday work acquainted them with failure, disappointment, scanty returns, hardship; the occasional bonanza, to be sure, but also much drudgery and more than a little danger. This is the fisherman's lot.

I learned of the rigours of commercial fishing when I was posted to a seacoast village upon ordination. Lobster, cod and mackerel were fished in boats with three feet of freeboard on the sides when frigid North Atlantic waves were ten feet high. Those who fished smelt used a chain saw to cut a slot in the winter ice 30 feet long, two feet wide, and as deep as the ice was thick (five feet). They dropped a weighted net into the slot and then pulled it up several hours later. Smelt have to be fished on the change of tide: 2:37 am, 4:15 pm, 3:10 am, and so on. For only pennies per pound these fellows endured constantly interrupted sleep and 75 kilometre per hour winds blowing off the North Atlantic at temperatures of -40°C. One night a salmon fisherman hooked onto an 800-pound tuna. Excitedly he brought it ashore and spent hours removing head and entrails — only to learn that mercury contamination might be unacceptably high in a fish that large. A Federal Fisheries officer confiscated it. The fisherman was heartbroken. Do you know what he did the next night? He put back to sea and fished again!

When Jesus called the twelve he could have appointed dreamers, speculators, visionaries, political sophisticates, academicians, or even religious experts. Such people were available. Instead he called those whom hardship, disappointment, fatigue and undeflectable persistence had already prepared for the greater work ahead of them.

In obedience to Jesus, Peter went deeper and let down the nets despite the fact that at face-value Christ's command seemed futile:

it was daytime and fish were caught at night and in shallower water. Yet Peter obeyed even when it seemed to invite failure.

But then Abraham had obeyed when the sacrifice of Isaac would have meant the failure of the very promise of God that had sustained him: "Your descendants shall be as numberless as the sands of the seashore." Moses obeyed the command to lead even as he knew his appearance and manner engendered failure. (How much leadership could a public figure exercise today when afflicted with glaring disabilities?) Naaman had obeyed — "bathe in the filthy river" — when to do so seemed to prevent the very cleansing he craved.

In the midst of a secularized age which writes off the church and its message, Christians must not only go deeper, shunning vague religious "smarm" and obsolete sentimentality; they must also recover and then hold up obediently the irreducible, irreplaceable truth and substance of the gospel, even while that gospel is ignored. Further, they must do all of this with the patience, resilience and persistence of fisherfolk who do not quit despite scanty returns, relentless hardship and ineradicable risk. Only as we do this shall we know ourselves to be precisely what our Lord has appointed us to be: fishers of men. Only as we hold all this together will the day come once again when the gospel is cherished for what it is: the power of God unto that salvation which everyone needs in any era.

A startling success

In Mark's account the disciples obeyed Jesus and immediately were met with what appeared to be startling success. They had fished in vain; now they were inundated with fish. Yet Peter responded in a manner that startles us: "Depart from me, for I am a sinful man." Peter knew there was nothing in him that merited what his Lord had done before his very eyes. The miracle he had witnessed was not a reward for either secret virtue or manifest rectitude which he possessed; it was the sheer gift of God. It humbled him as he had never been humbled before. The holiness of God highlighted Peter's depravity, and he could only confess himself to be a sinner through-and-through.

Not so long ago a man informed me exuberantly that he would have given everything to have been with Moses when God gave him the Ten Commandments. But of course the man wouldn't have been thrilled at all; he would have been terrified. Everywhere in scripture fear engulfs the people before whom the all-holy God has loomed. This fear is not a sign of a craven spirit or a fragile ego, never mind a neurosis. It is a sign of uncommon spiritual depth that finally recognizes the horror of its own sinnership.

Reawakening to sin

Another manifestation of the church's "going deeper" will be the church's reawakening to the human condition, even to the church's own sinnership. Christians will then be less quick to identify sin in others than to stand aghast at the breadth and penetration of their *own* depravity. Peter doesn't come to see, with a measure of sober insight, that there is this or that about him, whether motive or deed, that is unworthy of the master; he blurts his unendurable awareness that sin is *all* he has to admit.

Of course it is the self-giving One incarnate who steeps Peter in self-horror. In precisely the same way it will be love, and nothing but love, that exposes on the Day of Judgement what has been hidden in our hearts. To assume that judgement means God is resentful or a grudge-holder is as false as it is shallow. Profounder people know that love searches, convicts and horrifies as nothing else can. When the love of him who *is* Love (John 4:8) exposes my apparent altruism as subtle manipulation, when the kindness of God exposes my seeming sensitivity as fear of not being commended, when love's intensity unmasks my generous smile as the cloak for the vindictive spirit I am embarrassed to display — what can this produce in me except horror that cries, "Depart from me!"? If my wife loved me only slightly, then excuses for my treatment of her would be readier-to-hand and considerably more believable. As it is, the very love that sustains me shames me. Can God's greater love do any less?

A church that "goes deeper" will also know that its Lord does not leave us here. No sooner does Peter cry out in anguish than Jesus comforts him, "Fear not!" Everywhere in scripture where

God is met and fear consumes, the pronouncement "Fear not!" is heard immediately. It is a command of God, to be sure, but only because it is first and last God's *gift*. In commanding us to "fear not" God is turning us to face him, recognize his love and acknowledge his mercy as he quells in us that fear we should otherwise never be rid of.

Moments of appalling self-disgust lapped at John Newton for the rest of his life. He couldn't forget what he had unleashed through the slavetrade and was now powerless to prevent. Newton's heart was one with Peter's when the eighteenth-century Anglican wrote,

> Twas grace that taught my heart to *fear*
> And grace my fears *relieved*.

The church that beckons winsomely to a secular society is one that has ceased speaking of sin in terms of trivia and instead both recognizes profoundly the predicament of humankind and also glories gratefully in the love that unmasks us only to remake us.

To leave and to follow

It was the "relieved" disciples who came ashore and were told that henceforth they would "catch" others. Whereupon they left everything and followed Jesus. The crowds, meanwhile, had remained on the shore, and remained hungry as well for that Word they wanted to hear inasmuch as they couldn't generate it for themselves. It was as Peter and his friends "left" and "followed" that the crowds would be nourished with the bread of life.

Note: to "leave everything" and follow Jesus meant a change of livelihood for Peter and his colleagues. But it didn't mean this for others. They could follow as devotedly (and indeed were called to follow) while remaining a tentmaker (Paul), an officer of the city council (Erastus), a seamstress (Dorcas), an entrepreneur (Lydia), a royal attendant (the unnamed Ethiopian). The many who were like them followed Jesus every bit as devotedly as the few who ceased their customary employment.

Yet, in the course of following they had in fact "left everything." To "leave everything" is to leave behind an entire world, with its distorted outlook, grasping self-preoccupation, narcissistic self-promotion, and ludicrous confidence that it alone is reality when in fact it is devoid of substance and hastening towards death. It is to embrace that renewed universe our Lord has brought with him in being raised from the dead.

Upon coming to faith and joining Christ's people in Corinth, Erastus remained the city-treasurer. He now lived in a new world. Accordingly, while he was considerably more affluent than most others in the Corinthian congregation, he would not think himself superior to them; neither would he exploit his social privilege and "lord" it over them or manipulate them. At the same time the non-Christians in Corinth would know he could be counted on to bring integrity to the job: public monies would not be siphoned off for personal gain or private ventures. That world had been left behind forever.

Lydia, a businesswoman who handled carriage-trade women's clothing, was the first European convert on Paul's mission. She bore witness to the gospel with the result that her household (family and employees) cherished the Word and were baptized. In first-century Europe hotels were largely places of a reputation better left undescribed. To extend hospitality promptly and graciously, as Lydia did, declared one's recognition and repudiation of what the hotel-trade represented; it proved you now lived in a world renewed at God's hand.

Prisca and Aquila were tentmakers. Paul was everlastingly grateful for these two who had risked their necks for him. (Surely to risk death is to "leave all.") What's more, this Christian couple were Jewish. They had saved from untimely death the man who spoke of himself as "the apostle to the gentiles." For this reason "*all* the churches of the gentiles were to give thanks" for them (Romans 16:4). In addition, they opened up their home so that a house-church could gather there on Sundays. Their courage, as well as open hand, open heart and open home, plus the boost they gave the gentile mission — it all points to people who have "left everything" in order to follow.

Jesus insists his followers leave everything, for otherwise "following" will be more of the order of meandering, flipflopping, or lurching. The instability of it all is corrected, according to James, by one thing: single-mindedness.

Søren Kierkegaard said it with unique pithiness: "Purity of heart is to will one thing." To leave all and follow is to resolve that henceforth the sole good we pursue is the kingdom of God; the one word which orients us in the midst of dizzying confusion is the truth of the gospel; the one lord to whom we cling is Jesus Christ; and the reward which exhilarates us as nothing else is to have others join us in single-minded discipleship as they too are "caught" through the witness of those who have gone ever so deep themselves.

The day will come, in our secularized society, when in response to those who have "gone deeper" God will honour their diligence, patience and suffering. The day will come when people will press forward once again to hear the Word of God.

WINTER

The Wonder of God's Word

While the pressures of the wilderness may cause us to
feel we've been buried, the selfsame pressures can drive
us to God's Word, there to discover that to be
buried is to be given opportunity to burrow.
Having immersed ourselves in the gospel we shall
emerge into the radiance of God's new day.

Chapter 12

Psalm 13:
OF CONFLICTS,
CONTENDING, AND A CROWN

All who aspire to godliness should steep themselves in the Psalms.

Many of the Psalms are a cry to God to vindicate his own name. When "how long?" echoes in our hearts, we are to contend with God, holding him accountable for the promises he has made to us in our need. The Puritans used to speak of "sueing the mercies of the covenant-making God."

When I was a youngster I began reading the Psalms simply because I had been told it would do me good. The Psalms were the "prayerbook of the Bible"; it was important I learn to pray rightly, as this would help render me godly. Therefore all who aspired to godliness should steep themselves in the Psalms. I believed this then; I believe it now. I read the Psalms every day.

When I first read them, however, I was disturbed: the psalmist spoke of his enemies so very often that I wondered if the fellow weren't paranoid. What's more, he called down God's wrath so often that I wondered if he weren't vindictive. I didn't think I was going to be rendered godly by taking to heart someone who seemed both paranoid and vindictive, and so I left off reading the Psalms. I returned to them only when I was acquainted with two facts. First, where God's judgement is invoked upon our enemies it is recognized that our enemies are ours only because they are first God's. Our true enemies are not those who irk us or dislike us; they are first of all enemies of God's truth, purpose, way, faithfulness, patience and steadfast love. Second, what underlies God's invocation isn't mean-spirited vindictiveness but rather a plea for God to vindicate his own name; a plea for him to act so as to clear his own name of the slander God's enemies have heaped upon it.

As soon as I had these two facts straight the Psalms (and indeed the older testament as a whole) came alive for me as never before. I read it with renewed enthusiasm, relish and profit. It behooves all of us to return to the Psalms again and again that they might be imprinted upon us indelibly.

When enemies gloat

Psalm 13 is especially appropriate to our wanderings in the wilderness. "How long, O Lord?" the psalmist asks four times in two verses. "How long do I have to wait? How long must pain and sorrow torment me? How long shall my enemies *be exalted over me*?" His enemies — arrogant, puffed-up swaggerers — were gloating over him. They snickered at him, bragging of the humiliation they had forced upon him.

But because his enemies were first God's enemies, the psalmist was most upset not because he was visited with contempt, but because *God* was. His consternation merely reflected the distress that afflicted the heart of God.

Nonetheless, the psalmist himself was in pain; his enemies, while certainly God's first, were still his. In fact, so upset was he that he cried, "How long?" three more times. "How long am I to be stuck with this ache in my gut? How long will you, O Lord, hide your face from me?"

One reason I love the Psalms is that every predicament of the Christian is reflected in them. To be a Christian is to be surrounded with the enemies of our Lord himself. To be a Christian is to be immersed in conflict.

One of the saccharine myths that the church, ignorant of scripture, has foisted on Jesus, is that wherever he went people became agreeable. I regularly receive denominational literature which tells me (incorrectly) that because Jesus is the reconciler, his word and deed invariably reconcile people. No! Jesus is the reconciler, and therefore his word and deed *reconcile repentant sinners to God.* Our Lord doesn't reconcile the unrepentant; his word and deed *harden* them in their enmity to God. Our Lord *does* not, *cannot,* reconcile sin and righteousness, depravity and godliness, the evil one and the Holy One of Israel. These are everywhere and always irreconcilable.

Jesus the agitator

Before our Lord reconciles anyone to God he is the agitator who overturns everything. He was born in Bethlehem, a nondescript suburb of Jerusalem — and King Herod slew every male infant he could find. He began his public ministry by submitting to baptism at the hands of his cousin John — and John was executed. He preached in Capernaum and the people wanted to throw him over a cliff. He traveled to Jerusalem and the ecclesiastical bureaucracy plotted his demise. Finally he was betrayed by someone belonging to the most intimate circle of his followers. All of this I read in scripture. Yet the most recent document my denomination has published on scripture maintains that everywhere Jesus goes everyone becomes agreeable. In John's gospel, several times over, after Jesus has spoken or acted, we are told, "The people were divided." Before Jesus reconciles he fosters division, for he must first expose the enemies of God. Someone with no previous scriptural familiarity would see this upon first reading. Then why can't the church? Because a saccharine myth has obscured the truth of God.

Immersed in conflict

Some time ago I was asked to speak to a grade seven/eight class in an elementary school of the Toronto Board of Education. In the classroom was a large poster immediately beside the blackboard, where students couldn't help seeing it. The poster had to do with health matters. In huge letters it urged students, "B.Y.O.C." — "Bring Your Own Condom." Let us make no mistake: in any communication there are implicit as well as explicit messages. Implicitly the poster poured out scores of messages concerning sexual activity and its relation (non-relation) to human intimacy. (It's quite plain that those who approved the poster for the classroom see no connection at all between sexual activity and human intimacy.) Another of the many messages is that promiscuity is just fine; it's only disease that's bad. The poster's many implicit messages contradict what Christians believe about human intimacy and the manner in which sexual activity subserves it. The gospel informs us that marriage, the fusion of husband and wife, is like a tree graft: each component of the graft grows into the other so as to form a union that is finally indescribable. Moreover, as this union develops and matures and bears fruit, the intensified union itself is the fruit which results from the tree-graft. All of this was denied by the poster.

The teacher or parent who objects to it is going to be plunged into conflict instantly. Not to object, however, is to submerge one's convictions. To object will bring down the accusation of prudery, narrowness, naiveness, as well as a charge of being quarrelsome and prickly. Nonsense. It doesn't mean we're ornery and hard-to-get-along-with. To object, from a Christian perspective, means we will not deny our Lord; we will not say of our only Saviour and hope, "I don't know him now and never have." From a social perspective it means we will not allow or encourage a tail to wag the dog. From an educational perspective it means we have identified some aspects of the offerings of the Toronto Board of Education to be delusive and dangerous. It would most certainly plunge us into conflict.

I was formerly involved in another hotbed of conflict as president of The Peel Mental Health Housing Coalition and chairman of its board of directors. This organization attempts to procure housing for people who are chronically mentally ill. The Peel District Health Council had commissioned the Mental Health Housing Coalition to oversee the delivery of adequate housing for all mentally ill persons in the region of Peel. One aspect of the Housing Coalition's mandate is dealing with community resistance.

In previous years there was tremendous resistance concerning housing for the disadvantaged. Can you imagine the resistance that boiled up concerning housing for the deranged? It was inconceivable that I "duck" it, for to avoid the conflict would only be to betray defenseless people whom God does not betray.

Most church people have been told from age three that Jesus is nice, and therefore all good Christian people should be nice too. When theological betrayals first came upon our denomination a few years ago people quickly saw that to stand up for what they knew in their head and heart to be right would entail conflict. But Christians, they thought mistakenly, are conciliators, not contenders. And so across the country they largely capitulated, and one more tail — an unrighteous tail — was allowed to wag the dog. The terrible mistake by which they were victimized, the critical hinge on which everything turns in this pseudo-Christian view, is just this: Jesus isn't nice. Our Lord is many things, but he is not nice!

The psalmist was not surrounded by enemies because he himself had gone out of his way to antagonize people, or because he had a prickly, belligerent personality. He was surrounded by enemies inasmuch as God had drawn him into his own way, wisdom and truth. To remain faithful to the Holy One who cannot be deflected from his own righteousness is to be plunged into ceaseless conflict.

It's easy to understand this with our head. But understanding it makes it no easier for our heart to endure. For God's enemies, now our enemies, gloat; they taunt, strut, ridicule, misrepresent, disdain, lie. Before long we are crying with the psalmist, "How long is this going to last? How long are you going to hide your face from me?"

Hold God to his promises!

What happens next? We do what the psalmist did. He prayed. I don't mean he folded his hands and said prettily, "Dear saccharine One, help me to be saccharine too!" He shouted at God, "Consider me! Answer me! Aid me! But don't leave me stumbling around punch-drunk! Don't leave me in the dark so that my enemies taunt me all the more, 'Not only is he a fool, he is a God-forsaken fool!'"

"Consider me! Answer me! Do something!" These are *imperatives*. Is it not a little inappropriate as well as dangerous to address God this way? No! Everywhere in scripture to pray is to strive with God. When Jacob wrestled through the night, so intense was his struggle that he thought he was wrestling with another human being. In the morning, exhausted, he learned he was struggling with God. As a sign of this he would hobble the rest of his life, and his name was changed from Jacob ("deceiver") to Israel ("he who struggles with God"). When Hannah pleaded with God ardently and unselfconsciously Eli, a priest, said to her, "Woman, you are drunk. Put the cork back in the bottle." Hannah replied, "I am not drunk. I am a woman sorely troubled. I have been pouring out my soul before the Lord."

Our Israelite foreparents no more thought prayer should be pretty than they thought Jesus to be nice. Think of our Lord in Gethsemane. The English text tells us Jesus "knelt" in the garden. Ever after we've seen pictures of Jesus kneeling beside a flat-topped rock, hands folded serenely. The Greek text, however, uses a verb-tense that suggests Jesus fell to his knees, got up, fell down again, over and over, like someone beside himself. Paul told the Christians in Ephesus that when he prayed for them he said, "I bow my knees." He didn't mean he knelt down to pray (Jews always stand up to pray); he meant that his knees gave out, so intense was his intercession.

One of the words the New Testament uses to describe prayer is *agonizesthai* (from which we get our English word, "agonize"). It means to contend with the utmost exertion, to strive without letup, to wrestle without reserve. This is what it is to pray.

And this is what we do when conflict abounds and enemies gloat. We cry to God, "Consider me! Answer me! Aid me! But don't fall asleep on me or I will sleep the sleep of death while my enemies rejoice over me. For then they will think they have triumphed over you!"

Keep on contending

How do people find it in themselves to cry to God like this? How do they contend with enemies and keep on contending? The psalmist tells us: "I have trusted in God's steadfast love; my heart shall rejoice in God's salvation. I will sing to him, for he has dealt bountifully with me." All of this the psalmist put at the end of Psalm 13 to explain how he could contend with enemies and cry to God day after day. While he put it at the end, logically it comes at the beginning. It is the ground of everything the psalmist did.

God has dealt bountifully with me. I am a sinner who merits nothing from God; nothing, that is, apart from condemnation. Yet in his Son God has made provision for me and by his Spirit he has made that provision mine. If today the most hideous thing were to befall me it would still be the case that God has dealt bountifully with me. Of his incomprehensible mercy he has quickened in me that faith by which I am bound to him eternally. Then how could I ever say that he has dealt miserably with me or that I have been shortchanged? People are shortchanged anywhere in life when they don't get what they feel they are entitled to. But such is God's steadfast love for me that he has poured out on me everything I don't deserve (that salvation in which I rejoice) while sparing me everything I do deserve. Then how could I ever capitulate in those conflicts which are his first? Since he has dealt so bountifully with me as to save me, I owe him everything, particularly that faithfulness that but dimly reflects his faithfulness to me.

As surely as God *has* dealt bountifully with us he will *continue* to deal bountifully with us. Therefore we shall continue to trust in his steadfast love and rejoice in his salvation. We know that as often as our enemies harass us and we're driven to cry to God, he will hear us when we shout, "How long?" More than this, God will hasten the day when, in the words of Psalm 110, God makes his enemies his footstool. On that day his enemies will vanish forever, and therefore ours as well. Having trusted in his steadfast love, and rejoicing in his salvation, we shall glorify him for ever and ever.

The apostle James tells us that to remain faithful in the midst of conflict is to be honoured with that crown which God has promised to all who love him.

Chapter 13

Romans 12:

THE MOTIVATION OF GOD'S MERCY

*With eyes wide open to God's mercy
we can see our way clear to serve.*

*What gets us on our feet
and into the "field"
faster than gratitude for
what God has done
for us? Our awareness of
God's astounding mercy
sobers us and frequently
silences us but never
immobilizes us.*

What moves the Christian to live like a Christian? The ground of all that we do is simply God's mercy. Our motivation to live like a Christian is gratitude for this mercy.

This truth was expressed by the apostle Paul who was dramatically apprehended by God on the road to Damascus. To the new convert it was never enough that the gospel be understood and believed; it had to be lived.

In Paul's earlier chapters in his treatise to the Romans he has expounded the riches of the gospel: how God makes sinful people right with himself, why all humankind needs to be made right with God, the manner in which the gospel quickens faith in people and binds them to Christ. Then beginning in chapter 12 he tells his readers how the gospel is to be lived in their day-to-day affairs. The first thing Paul puts forward in this section is the ground of our doing anything at all.

J.B. Phillips, the best paraphraser of the New Testament, begins Romans 12, "With your eyes wide open to the mercies of God . . ." Christians are those who have intimate acquaintance with the mercy of God. We know ourselves liberated, renewed and invigorated at God's own hand. I know I am the beneficiary of God's mercy. I've known since I was nine years old that as sinner I merited only condemnation, that the amnesty God fashioned for me I didn't deserve. Therefore it had to be rooted in his mercy alone. Mercy is love poured out on those who merit no love at all and never will. That I live at all is a manifestation of God's mercy. That I have been rendered a new creature in Christ Jesus, sustained in this newness every day by God's Spirit and destined for eternal glory — this is an even greater manifestation of mercy. It is this greater mercy that will always be the rock-bottom truth and reality of my life. Ceaseless gratitude will ever be the only worthy motivation of my Christian conduct.

Our awareness of God's astounding mercy certainly sobers us and frequently silences us, but it never immobilizes us. On the contrary, says the apostle Paul, our awareness of God's mercy moves us to offer our bodies to God as a living sacrifice.

Our bodies, our selves

Our bodies? How do I offer my body to God? Paul means my self. I don't avoid offering this or that about myself, as though I were trying to get off cheap with God; I offer my self, all of my self. Then why does the apostle say "body"? Because he is a Jew, and the Hebrew mind knows there is no human self apart from a body. I have no self apart from my body. If my friend phones me up and asks, "Would you like to play baseball this afternoon?" I don't reply, "Sure, I'd love to. I'll bring along my ball and glove; I'll bring along my body too." It would be nonsensical inasmuch as "I" can't play baseball apart from my body. Neither can I honour or obey God without my body. My personhood, my identity, my innermost "I" is inseparable from it.

The last several years have acquainted us with notorious scandal among television preachers who thought they could honour and serve God apart from their bodies. "They" could serve God while their bodies were off doing something else. Those men disgraced themselves. My gratitude to God for my salvation must ever move me to offer God my body, my self, all of me without qualification or reservation.

My offering all of "me" to God is "spiritual worship," says Paul. Some translations say "reasonable service," others, "spiritual worship." The Greek expression means both, and I'm sure Paul had both meanings in mind. It's reasonable in that my obedient service to God is the only reasonable response to his mercy that has saved me. At the same time, my aspiration to live the gospel is the only sign that my spirituality is authentically Christian.

What it all adds up to, says the apostle, is that we're not to be conformed to the world. We're not to let the world squeeze us into its mould.

In the latter part of the 12th chapter Paul tells us our Christian existence unfolds in the world. Christians are committed to the world. We're not to try to live in a little religious ghetto that shuts out the big, bad world. At the same time, the very world we are to live in and struggle for is a world to which we are not to conform.

Our first sphere of service

In the middle part of chapter 12 Paul speaks of our Christian service to the church. Before you and I are qualified to serve the world we must serve the church. Of course! Surely our fellow-Christians have first claim upon us. After all, it is they who nurture, encourage and sustain us. They must have first claim upon us, since we don't hesitate to look to them for whatever we need whenever we need it. Furthermore, if we're unable to serve our fellow-Christians in the church (where we share a common Lord, common faith, common hope) how shall we fare in the wider world (which is meaner, tougher, more resistant, and utterly unforgiving)? The first sphere of our service is always the church.

In our service to the church Paul insists we shun exaggerated ideas of ourselves or our importance. Paul makes this point first because he knows that the church gives people the chance to be a big toad in a small pond; and not merely a big toad, a totalitarian toad. Compared to where our lives unfold during the week the local congregation is small. The person who has no clout in his place of employment finds he has immense clout in a congregation. What's more, congregations tend to be docile in the face of someone who speaks loudly or shrilly. As we've noted, most church people have grown up with the idea that they should be nice inasmuch as Jesus was nice. C.S. Lewis maintains that according to the New Testament Jesus is tender and terrifying in equal parts, but never "nice." Still, when a powerplay unfolds in congregational life or someone browbeats another member, others decide quickly they should acquiesce in order to keep things nice. The noisy browbeater or the powerplay specialist wins the day. The big toad in the small pond is now even bigger.

The apostle is aware of this. For this reason he says up front: "Don't think more highly of yourself than you ought to think." This is foundational. Without it church life will fragment.

Exercising our gifts

Paul next tells us that each of us is to exercise, for the good of the congregation, whatever ministry we have been given to exercise. Our ministry, or service, is simply the exercising of the gifts we have.

He is careful to note three things: first, *every* Christian has a service to render the believing community, just because every Christian has a gift. Second, we should exercise only those gifts we have; we shouldn't attempt to exercise gifts we don't have. This is why he says, "If your gift is teaching, then teach (don't attempt carpentry); if your gift is exhortation or encouragement, then exhort or encourage." Very often in church life we expect people to exercise gifts they manifestly do not have. Then we're surprised when an important task in church life goes undone or is done poorly; surprised again when the person who attempted to do it feels guilty at having done it so poorly. We are to do only what has been given us to do. We should never feel guilty for not doing what we have no gift for doing.

Third, whatever our service is, we're to render it wholeheartedly, generously, zealously, cheerfully. We're not to render it stingily or miserably. "Whoever contributes, liberally; whoever gives assistance, enthusiastically; whoever does acts of mercy, cheerfully." There is nothing as destructive as "doing good," so-called, that is done reluctantly, resentfully, grudgingly. Congregational life thrives when everyone's service is recognized and encouraged in a spirit of magnanimity. Not only is congregational life made to thrive, says the apostle, Christians are at this point qualified for their service to the world.

Collision with the world

Regarding our service to the world (v. 14) Paul says, "Bless those who persecute you; bless them, don't curse them." Doesn't that wake you up? The service Christians render the world for the sake of the world, the world throws back in the Christian's face! This is because the world the Christian must serve is precisely that world to which the Christian must not conform. Right off the bat, then, there is going to be a collision.

At this point the Christian is always tempted to protect himself by turning his back on the world and huddling in a corner with a blanket pulled over his head. The apostle forbids this because he knows his Lord forbids it. (After all, says St. John, it is the world God so loved that he broke himself for it.) We're not to stand aloof. In fact, says Paul, we're to stand so close to the world, in such solidarity with other people, that we rejoice with those who rejoice and weep with those who weep. We weep inasmuch as we're sensitive to their hurt and care for them in the midst of their pain; we rejoice inasmuch as we do not envy whatever it is that has made them rejoice, and therefore do not jealously dash cold water on their elation.

Moreover, the apostle insists we're not to be haughty, but rather we're to associate with the lowly. J.B Phillips again: "Don't become snobbish, but take a real interest in ordinary people."

Nothing has the capacity to foster pride or secret arrogance like belonging to an elite. It can be academic, professional, athletic or religious. There is certainly nothing wrong with belonging to such elites. Why shouldn't the academically gifted person enjoy the company of other academics, the athlete the company of fellow-athletes, and so on? At the end of the day, however, everyone who belongs to the most elevated elite is in exactly the same condition as those who belong to no elite at all: everyone is a suffering human being, fragile, lonely, sinful, facing bodily and mental dissolution — and aware of all of this together with the awareness of spiritual impoverishment. Everyone is subject to the same heartaches, guilt and apprehension. The Christian is to "take a real interest in ordinary people" because everyone is ultimately ordinary. At bottom our need is the same and the gospel is the same. We are alike sinners and sufferers who stand empty-handed before God and need what he alone can give us.

The last thing Paul tells us in Romans 12 about our participation in the world's life is that we're never to seek revenge. Once we have recognized our enemy we do not launch a vendetta against him that will only ruin us before it ever ruins him. Vengeance is never our responsibility simply because as soon as we are stabbed we lose perspective. Judgement must be left in the hands of him who is always the just judge. Our responsibility is to mirror that truth and mercy which have made us who we are. To do anything else is to be overcome by evil when, says Paul in the very last sentence of Romans 12, our task is always, and only, to overcome evil with good.

Chapter 14

Ephesians 6:
CERTAIN ARMOUR FOR UNCERTAIN TIMES

Discipleship is not warfare only, but warfare always.

Daily we must resolve to think and act as a servant and soldier of Jesus Christ. We need life-long armour for the task. God has not co-opted us for a work bee, but has conscripted us for warfare. Nothing less than the whole armour is needed.

The apostle Paul frequently used military metaphors to explain the Christian faith. He did so in order to render our discipleship more resilient and of greater service to our Lord. This was perhaps strange in that the Roman soldier was the most hated person in first-century Palestine. He personified everything Jewish people hated about the occupation and its detestable army. Not only had Jewish people been deprived of political self-determination, they had to be reminded of it every time the uniformed soldier marched by. In addition, they couldn't do a thing about the arbitrary power the soldier wielded. If a soldier barked, "Carry my pack!" you put down your bag of groceries as fast as you could, said, "Yes, sir" and carried his pack for as long and as far as he told you. Otherwise he might just tickle your tonsils with his sword.

What grated most on Jewish people, however, was the Roman disregard of everything Jewish people held sacred, such as the temple in Jerusalem. Only the high priest entered the Holy of Holies, the innermost room of the temple, and then only once per year, on the Day of Atonement. General Pompey, however, tramped around in it in his muddy boots, then walked back outside with a smirk and announced he hadn't seen a thing in the unadorned cubby-hole, never mind the God Jews were always talking about. He made no secret of the fact that as far as he was concerned the Holy of Holies was of no more significance than an outhouse. Roman soldiers were loathed.

Nevertheless, whenever Jesus spoke of them in the course of his earthly ministry he spoke well of them. A Roman officer said to him, "I am an officer; when I speak people jump. You have authority too; I know you have. My servant is sick unto death; if you but speak the word your word will free him and he will be healed." Jesus looked around at the crowd of spectators who were disgusted that he would even speak to a soldier and said to them, "I haven't found anything approaching this fellow's faith among the lot of you, and you think you're God's favourites!"

Needless to say no Jew, and therefore no Jewish Christian, would ever have wanted to join the Roman army. But no gentile Christian could. All Roman soldiers had to promise unconditional loyalty to the emperor, and no Christian could agree to this. Isn't it startling, then, that since soldiering was alien to both Jewish and gentile Christians, the apostles used pictures from soldiering to speak of Christian discipleship! Paul especially compared following Jesus to military existence. Plainly he admired much about the men whom everyone else despised; he saw many aspects of soldiering the Christian must take to heart.

Trained to fight

In examining military metaphors we see, first of all, that a soldier is trained to fight. A soldier may and will do other things, such as help civilians in times of natural disaster or search for lost children; but these tasks are ancillary to the preeminent task of fighting. In the same way discipleship isn't fighting only (there are other things we do); nevertheless, discipleship is fighting always. Faith never ceases having to fight.

Faith — yours and mine — has to be contended for every day. To be sure faith is God's gift; we can never bestow it upon ourselves. At the same time, faith is that for which we must struggle and contend. Every day faith is assaulted, and therefore every day I must resolve afresh that I am going to think, believe, do as a servant and soldier of Jesus Christ. Not to fight for faith every day is to succumb to despair; not to contend for it is to fall into hopelessness; it is to surrender to the world's way of thinking, believing and doing; it is to "go with the flow," drift downstream, finally drift on out where the lost are drowned.

This isn't to say each day brings relentless intensity to the struggle. Some days are intense, but many more are much less so. Still there are no days when the Christian can coast. If we are unconvinced we must fight for faith then we should look at our Lord himself. First in the wilderness, where he is tested to the breaking point: is he going to deceive the people with bread and circuses and guarantee himself a popularity he would never have by holding up the way of the cross? Is there a pain-free shortcut to the kingdom of God? Is obedience to his Father no more demanding than a snooze in a rocking chair? Then see our Lord again in Gethsemane: sweat pours off his forehead as though he had received a fifty-stitch gash. Then see him on the cross. He quotes Psalm 22, which begins, "My God, my God, why have you forsaken me?" As he hangs he is still fighting for faith. He knew what he was doing when he cited Psalm 22 as his affirmation of faith, for verse 24 declares, "God has not despised or abhorred the affliction of the afflicted, and God has not hid his face from the afflicted one, but God has heard when the afflicted one cried to God." Our Lord's confidence in his Father is undiminished at the last; but what a struggle to get to the last!

Henry Farmer, a British philosopher whom I read in my undergraduate days, was preaching on God's love in an English church during World War II. A Polish fellow who had escaped to England when Poland was overrun waited behind to see Farmer after the service. "Like you, I know what it is to be loved by God," the

Polish man said. "Unlike you, however, I know what it is to struggle for it when the blood of one's dearest friends is running in the gutter on a cold winter's morning."

I have sat with tragedy-racked people whose tragedy should have rendered faith forever impossible, according to the psychologists. Yet they hung on, groped for a while, floundered a while longer, began to claw their way out of the emotional rubble which seemed to be suffocating them, and persisted until they could finally say with Job, "Though he slay me, yet will I trust him."

Paul writes to Timothy, a younger minister, "Fight the good fight of faith; take hold of the eternal life to which you were called; seize this life!" The apostle does not say, "Fight *a* good fight," which would mean, "Give it a good go, my boy, and do your best." He says "Fight *the* good fight of faith." Faith is the fight we shall always have to wage in a world of unbelief, a world that forever wants to render us blind, impotent unbelievers ourselves.

Faith is not only that which we must fight *for*; it's also that which we must fight *from*. It's the standpoint from which we fight as we contend with everything that hammers us day-by-day. Christians, possessed by the One who is ultimate reality, engage a world of falsehood and illusion. Clinging to the righteousness of Christ, we are immersed in the world's morass of sin, both subtle and shabby. Desiring no other leader than the one who has made us his through his costliest mercy, we journey with him in a world where he is either not recognized or not esteemed but in any case rarely espoused. Either we fight in this environment and thrive or we capitulate and disappear.

Peace at any price?

Another frequent misunderstanding which flows out of the "nice notion" about Jesus is that the Prince of Peace wants peace at any price. This of course is patently ridiculous since peace-at-any-price types never get crucified, since they never offend anyone. From the day his public ministry began Jesus was immersed in conflict without letup, as the sketchiest reading of the written gospels will disclose.

Yet because the misunderstanding persists — "Jesus calls us away from conflict" — conflict is the one thing that some church members fear above all else — even more than heresy, blasphemy, illogical gibberish, or even outright denial of our Lord. We fear conflict so much, and so dread a fight (not understanding, of course, that faith *is* a fight) that we will submerge convictions concerning holiness, righteousness and godliness. Congregational capitulation on matters congregations oppose in their hearts proves this.

The earliest and most elemental Christian confession is "Jesus is Lord." But you will look in vain for it in some church publications. In my denomination it's now deemed offensive (for many reasons) to say "Jesus is Lord." The earliest Christians knew better than we just how offensive it was: they were willing to die for it. I have watched lay-representatives from different congregations march off to area church meetings determined to speak up on behalf of the congregations that have commissioned them. They are ten minutes into the meeting when a leader (usually clergy) suggests that their outlook is narrow, bigoted, uninformed, cruel, anti-Christian. Either the lay-representative asserts himself or he caves in. If he asserts himself he has a fight on his hands; but all his life he's been told Christians don't fight; therefore he caves in — and unrighteousness has triumphed again. Of course the person who is always looking for a fight is sick; but the one who is always fleeing a fight is faithless. Before our Lord brings peace he brings conflict. His own ministry demonstrates this.

Since Christians cannot avoid life-long fighting we plainly need life-long armour. Paul explores the military metaphor once again, this time in his letter to the congregation in Ephesus, as he speaks of "the whole armour of God." We need the *whole* armour of God, all of it, if we're to do what he insists all Christians must do; namely, "withstand in the evil day." To be a Christian in the midst of "this present darkness" (Eph. 6:12) means that our Lord has not co-opted us for a "work bee"; he has conscripted us for warfare.

Essential support

The first item of armour the apostle mentions is *truth*. We are to gird our loins with truth. In first-century Palestine men wore an ankle-length garment. When a man "girded his loins" he reached back between his legs, pulled the back of his garment up between his legs and tucked it into his belt. He did this whenever he was about to work, run or fight. Battle dress for the Roman soldier, on the other hand (and Paul is thinking here of soldiers particularly), didn't include an ankle-length garment. Strictly speaking that which girded the soldier's loins wasn't part of his armour; it was the underwear he wore beneath his armour. (Precisely its nature I shall leave to your imagination. Suffice it to say no male athlete is ever found without it.) The loin-girder the Christian is always to be clothed in, says Paul, is truth. Truth is the Christian's underwear: not flaunted, not flashy, but essential support for those who have to fight.

When the apostle speaks of truth he has two meanings in mind: truth in the sense of truthfulness (transparency, straightforwardness), and truth in the sense of the verities of the faith, the substance of the faith, doctrine. The Christian's loins are to be girded with truth in both senses. We are possessed of the truth of faith, and we are transparent in attesting it before others.

In the ancient world the loins were regarded as the seat of strength and the seat of reproduction. It is only as the Christian is equipped with truth in both senses that the Christian herself remains strong in the evil day and that her witness gives birth to new Christians who do not fail to thrive in an inhospitable environment. Remember: before the Roman soldier put on a single piece of armour he put on his underwear; he girded his loins. The apostle insists that the most elemental aspect of the Christian's preparedness is a grasp of the truth and a truthfulness which is transparent to it.

The shield of faith

The single most important *defensive* item in the soldier's armour was the shield. "Take the shield of faith, with which you can quench all the flaming darts of the evil one." The worst military defeat a Roman army suffered occurred when enemy archers ignited their pitch-dipped arrows and fired one volley into the air, like modern-day mortar fire. These arrows rained down on the Roman troops as they held their shields above their heads. Whereupon the enemy archers fired a second volley straight ahead. The Roman soldiers could not protect themselves against attack from two directions at once. In addition, whatever flaming arrows they managed to block with their wooden shield promptly set their shield on fire and they had to drop it. Now they were completely defenseless and were slaughtered.

From how many directions is the Christian assaulted at once? And how many different flaming arrows are there? There is false guilt, imposed by a world that mocks Christians for being less than perfect. There is the self-accusation that lingers from an upbringing that thought magnifying a supposed sense of sin would magnify a sense of God's mercy, only to find that the latter never got magnified. There is the temptation that can fall on any one of us at any time and leave us weak-kneed, so vivid and visceral can temptation be. There is disillusionment as other Christians let us down, discouragement as we let ourselves down, bewilderment as we wonder how many more attacks we can sustain from how many more directions. Faith alone in our victorious Lord, says the apostle, will ever keep us from going down. We shall neither be burned up slowly by the flaming arrows nor be left bleeding to death quickly. The shield of faith finally defends Christ's people against everything which tends to sunder them from him.

The sword of the Spirit

The only offensive weapon Paul mentions is "the sword of the Spirit, which is the Word of God." The Christian individually and Christians collectively must ever wield the gospel *only*. The church of Jesus Christ must never coerce; our only offensive weapon is the Word of God (the gospel) in the power of the Spirit. If the advance of the gospel seems turtle-like and the power of the Spirit largely ineffective, too bad! The church has always behaved its worst when it forgot this and coerced people. It has coerced them militarily, economically and psychologically. Today I hear it lamented that in a secular era the church has no clout. Whoever said we were supposed to have clout? We are called to cross-bearing, not to clout-clobbering! After all, it is the crucified one who reminds disciples that no servant is above her master. Because the church is no longer in a position to coerce, Christ's people will have to learn what it is once again to have nothing more in our hand than Spirit-infused gospel.

In any case the Christian whose underwear is truth, whose defense is faith, and whose only offensive weapon is the gospel is equipped for anything that may befall him in the evil day.

Fighting will cease

If you grow weary of the military metaphor of fighting, be assured: relief is on the way. No soldier fights forever. The day when fighting is over comes sooner for some soldiers than for others, but one thing is certain: we shall not have to fight eternally. When Paul knew the Roman government was going to execute him, that he couldn't delay it any longer, he said simply, "I have fought the good fight, I have finished the race, I have kept the faith." His fighting days were over; he knew it, and he was glad of it.

How glad? He wrote to Timothy, "The time of my departure has come." "Departure" here translates *analusis*, a common Greek word for unhitching a draft horse from the wagon it had hauled throughout the heat of the day; no more toil to be endured, no more strain, just rest.

It was also the word for loosening the ropes of a tent. The apostle who had journeyed across Asia Minor and Europe was striking camp again, with one journey only in front of him, and nothing at all arduous or threatening about it.

It was also the word for unfastening the mooring ropes of a ship as the ship began its voyage home. Rest from fatiguing work, folding one's tent for the final journey, slipping one's moorings for the voyage home.

In a day when soldiering was despised the apostles followed our Lord in finding in soldiering a rich picture of Christian discipleship. We must fight the good fight of faith, fight for faith and fight from faith, every day. We must be equipped with the whole armour of

God, since we have to withstand in the evil day. Truth, faith and gospel are as much armour as we shall ever need. And then there comes the day when we shan't need any armour at all, for this time the soldier has gone home.

SPRING

Awakenings in the Wilderness

Only God can shake us out of our winter bleakness,
dreariness and barrenness, as he invigorates us with
his truth and frees us from our foolish "selfism."

Chapter 15

FORGIVING THE MAJOR AND MINOR LEAGUE SINNER

Spiritual awakenings must begin at the cross.

Forgiving enemies is the measure of our closeness to God. It must cost us something, as it cost God. Yet to forgive is not to advertise ourselves as a doormat, nor is it to shrug, "It doesn't matter."
Not to forgive ourselves is arrogance, even blasphemy.

Forgiveness: where to begin? We must start with the cross. The cross looms so large in the New Testament that it dominates the landscape. All theological understanding is rooted in it; all discipleship flows from it. It is what we trust for our salvation. It transfigures our thinking, distinguishing us from the mindset that bedevils the world.

To begin anywhere else means we've begun with calculating: "Should I forgive — self and others? How much should I forgive? Under what circumstances?"

Calculation in matters that concern us tends to serve our self-interest. You go to the bank to purchase your RRSP. The interest rates are 7% for one year, 7.25% for two, 7.5% for three. You estimate how the rate is going to fluctuate in the next few years, and calculate which combination and time period is best. Best for the bank? Of course not! Best for you.

Calculation is frequently a cover-up for rationalization. At a conscious level I calculate whether I should forgive, how much I should forgive, whom I should forgive. But all of this is a smoke-screen behind which there's an unconscious desire to even a score, to see someone who has pained me suffer a little more himself. Such rationalization, like any unconscious proceeding, is a process that spares us having to admit our own nastiness and to acknowledge what we prefer to hide. It cloaks deeper issues of sin and pride, yet leaves us thinking we are virtuous.

Moreover, calculation traffics in the unrealistic. What I am (virtuously) prepared to forgive in others will in fact be slight, what I expect others to forgive in me will in fact be enormous.

Calculation both presupposes and promotes shallowness. It encourages me to think sin is something I can calculate or measure like sugar, flour or milk.

We must begin with the cross; and more than begin, *stay* with the cross.

Nobody uses a 20-member surgical team to clip a hangnail. No government sends out a nuclear-powered aircraft carrier to sink a canoe. The air-raid warning isn't sounded because a child's paper glider has violated air-space. When the surgical team is deployed the patient's condition is critical. When the aircraft carrier puts to sea the impending threat couldn't be greater. When the warning is sounded destruction is imminent. When God gives up his own Son, humankind's condition is critical, the threat facing us couldn't be greater, our destruction is imminent.

What forgiveness means to God

As often as I read scripture I am sobered to read that God's forgiveness of you and me necessitated the death of God's own Son. I try to fathom what this means from the Father's perspective. Ponder the anguish of our foreparent in faith, Abraham, at Mount Moriah: his collecting the firewood, sharpening the knife, deflecting his young son's anxiety, trudging with leaden foot and heart up the side of the mountain. He and Sarah had waited years for a child and finally gave up. When everyone "just knew" the situation was hopeless, Sarah conceived. Was any child longed for more intensely or cherished more fervently? Now they had to give up this child, up to death.

I have been spared losing a child. I do know, however, that when a child dies the parents separate 70 percent of the time. Wouldn't the death bring the parents closer together? The truth is, so traumatic is the death of a child that calculation is useless; we cannot begin to comprehend what it is like, unless we have been there.

At the last minute a ram was provided. Abraham's relief was inexpressible. But when the Father of our Lord Jesus Christ walked his Son to Calvary *there was no relief for him.* Here the Father bore in his heart the full weight of that devastation.

Next I ponder what the cross means from the perspective of the Son. Without minimizing the physical suffering he endured for our sakes, I realize countless people have endured much greater physical pain. (It took him only six hours to die.) It's the dereliction that ices my bowels. What is it to be forsaken when the sum and substance of your life is unbroken intimacy with your Father?

As a child I was lost only two or three times. It wasn't a pleasant experience; in fact it was terrifying. Still, I knew my problem was simply that I couldn't find my parents; I never suspected for one minute that they had abandoned me. A man who is dear to me told me that when his wife left him and he knew himself bereft, forsaken by the one human being who meant more to him than all others, he turned on all the taps in the house so he wouldn't have to hear her driving out of the garage, driving out of his life. Before our Lord's Good Friday dereliction I can only fall silent in incomprehension.

As often as I begin with the cross I am stunned all over again at the price God paid — Father and Son together — for my forgiveness. In the same instant I'm sobered at the depravity in me that necessitated so great a price. It's plain that my depravity is oceans deeper than I thought, my heart-condition vastly more serious than I guessed. It is incontrovertible that when I have trotted out all my bookish, theological definitions of sin I still haven't grasped — shall never grasp — what sin means to God.

Father, forgive them . . .

As a teenager I thought our Lord to be wrong when he prayed for his murderers, "Father, forgive them, for they don't know what they are doing." It seemed to me they *did* know what they were doing: they were eliminating someone they didn't like. They had to know what they were doing simply because they had schemed and conspired to do it. Furthermore, I thought our Lord's plea self-contradictory. After all, if they didn't know what they were doing then they didn't need to be forgiven; they could simply be overlooked. Now I perceive our Lord was right. His assassins didn't know, ultimately, that they were crucifying the Son of God. They didn't know their sinnership had impelled them to do it. While they thought they were acting freely they were really in bondage because of their sinnership more surely than the cocaine sniffer is in bondage to dope. They cannot be excused; they can only be forgiven. They're blind to their own depravity, as we all are. But this doesn't lessen our accountability for it, as the day of judgement will make plain.

Why wait until then? Why not own the truth of the cross now? A cure so drastic presupposes a situation no less drastic; a cure whose blessing is richer than we can comprehend presupposes a condition whose curse is deadlier than we can imagine.

The measure of our closeness to God

Our understanding of forgiving ourselves and others unfolds from the cross. By its illumination we see everything else concerning forgiveness.

For instance, it is the consistent testimony of the apostles that forgiving our enemies is the measure of our closeness to God. When this truth first hit home I sank to the floor. Surely I could enjoy intimacy with God while enjoying the fantasy of my worst enemy going from misery to misery. Then in the light of the cross I saw that I couldn't. How could I claim intimacy with the One who forgives his assassins and at the same time relish ever-worsening misery for those who have not yet assassinated me? How can I say

I crave being recreated in the image of the God for whom forgiving costs him everything while I make sure that my non-forgiving costs me nothing?

Two hundred and fifty years ago John Wesley wrote in his journal, "Resentment at an affront is sin, and I have been guilty of this a thousand times." *We* want to say, "Resentment at an *imagined* affront would be sin, since it would be wrong to harbour resentment towards someone when that person had committed no real offense at all. But it would be entirely in order to harbour resentment at a real affront. After all, who wouldn't?" To argue like this, however, is only to prove we've not yet come within a country mile of the gospel. Resentment at an imagined affront wouldn't be sin so much as stupidity. Because resentment at a real affront comes naturally to fallen people we think it isn't sin. How can we ever be held accountable for something that fits us like a glove? But remember, the most serious consequence of our sinnership is our blindness to the fact, nature and scope of our sinnership.

Then what are we to do with our resentment? Do we hold it to us ever so closely because its smouldering heat will fuel our self-pity and self-justification? Or do we deplore it and drop it at the foot of the cross, knowing that only the purblind do anything else?

The unforgiving servant

Our Lord's parable of the unforgiving servant leaves us in no doubt or perplexity. The king forgives his servant a huge debt; the servant turns around and refuses to forgive a fellow whatever this fellow owes him. The king, livid that the pardon the servant received he does not in turn extend, orders the servant shaken up until some sense is shaken into him. If the servant had refused to forgive his fellow a paltry sum, he would merely have looked silly. But the amount he is owed isn't paltry; 100 denarii is six months' pay. Then the servant is readily understood, isn't he: the forgiveness required of him is huge. But the point of the parable is this: while the 100 denarii the servant is owed is no trifling sum, it is nothing compared to the 10,000 talents ($50 million) the king has already forgiven the servant.

That injury or offense you and I are to forgive is not a trifle. Were it a trifle we shouldn't be wounded. The wound is gaping; if it were anything else we shouldn't be sweating over forgiving it! We shall be able to forgive it only as we place it alongside what God has already forgiven in us. Note that we're never asked to generate forgiveness out of our own resources; we're simply asked not to impede God's forgiveness from flowing through us and spilling over onto others. We don't have to generate water in order for it to irrigate what is parched and render it fruitful; all we have to do is not put a crimp in the hose. Either we do not impede the free flow of God's forgiveness from him through us to others, or, like the servant in the parable, we shall have to be shaken up until some sense has been shaken into us.

What forgiveness doesn't mean

Forgiveness doesn't mean that the offense we are called to forgive is slight; it is grievous. Were it anything but grievous we should be talking about overlooking it instead of forgiving it.

It doesn't mean the offense is excused. To forgive is not to excuse. We excuse what is excusable. What is not and will never be excusable is also never excused; it can only be *forgiven*. The day you tell me you have forgiven me is the day I know I am without excuse. To forgive is never a shorthand version of, "Oh, it doesn't matter." To forgive is to say it matters unspeakably.

It doesn't mean we are suckers asking the world to victimize us again. To forgive is not to invite another assault or to advertise ourselves as a doormat. To be sure, some people are doormats, their self-image so poor and their ego-strength so diminished they seem to invite exploitation. Forgiveness, however, is not the last resort of the wimp who can't do anything else in any case. Rather, it's a display of ego-strength that couldn't be stronger. Jesus can forgive those who slay him just because he has already said, "No one takes my life from me; I may lay it down of my own accord, but *I* lay it down; no one takes it from me."

Forgiveness doesn't mean the person we forgive we regard as a diamond in the rough, a good-at-heart. It is to recognize that the person we forgive is depraved in heart and mind. After all, this is what God's forgiveness of us means about you and me.

It doesn't mean the person we must forgive we can therefore trust. Many people can never be trusted. The only people we should trust are those who show themselves trustworthy. Forgiveness does mean, however, that the person we cannot trust we shall yet not hate, abuse or exploit; we shall not plot revenge against him or bear him ill-will of any sort.

All that matters is that we not impede the forgiveness God has poured upon us and which he intends to course through us onto others.

Forgiving ourselves

But what about forgiving ourselves? Very often the person we most urgently need to forgive is ourselves. Since all forgiveness is difficult to the point of anguish, to forgive ourselves may be the most difficult of all.

Suppose we say, "I can forgive anyone at all except myself." What's going on in our head and heart?

Surely we have puffed up ourselves most arrogantly. There is terrible arrogance in saying to ourselves, "I am the greatest sinner in the world; the champion. I can forgive others because they are only minor-league sinners compared to me. When it comes to depravity I am the star of the major leagues."

Not only does a perverse arrogance underlie such an attitude, there is no little blasphemy as well. It is to say, "The blood-bought pardon of God, wrought at what cost to him we cannot fathom, isn't effective enough for me. Where I am concerned, God's mercy is deficient, defective, and finally worthless." Our forgiveness, which cost God we know not what, you and I shouldn't be labeling a garage-sale piece of junk.

If we say we cannot forgive ourselves we are likely wanting to flagellate ourselves in order to expiate our sin. But don't we believe the gospel? The heart of the gospel is this: *atonement has already been made for us.* We neither dismiss it nor add to it. We simply trust it.

And so we make full circle back to the cross, where we began. It is here we see that God, for Christ's sake, has forgiven us. Therefore we can do no other than forgive others, even ourselves.

Chapter 16

OF GRATITUDE AND GODLINESS

Life blossoms for those who are ceaselessly grateful.

We need to be turned out of ourselves, to look to the friends we don't deserve, the serendipities that surprise us, the unwearying patience of God, his ever-effervescing truth and fathomless mercy. Gratitude renders us holy and therefore profoundly healthy and happy.

"Just who do you think you are?" someone asked me recently. But the question wasn't nasty or hostile. It was asked in a spirit that was a peculiar blend of humour and seriousness. I felt the only thing for me to do was reply in the same spirit. "I think I am a mathematician-turned-grammarian," I replied, "because grammar is the key to life." The more I ponder my reply the more I think it was more serious than humorous: grammar is the key to life.

Think of Paul's mini grammar-lesson in 1 Thessalonians 5:16-18: "Rejoice always," "Pray constantly," "Give thanks in all circumstances." The mood of the verbs is imperative; the tense is present iterative. *Imperative* means we're commanded to do something; *iterative* means we're commanded to do it unremittingly. We are *always* to rejoice, *ceaselessly* to keep on praying, *unfailingly* to give thanks in all circumstances. We are to thank God from the moment we regain consciousness in the morning until that moment we fade out at night.

But note something crucial: the apostle tells us we're to thank God *in* all circumstances, not *for* all circumstances. We're never commanded to thank God for all circumstances. It would be the height of spiritual ignorance to do so for then we should be thanking God for those things he opposes.

Yet while not thanking God for everything we must thank him *in* everything, for there is no development in our lives where God is absent or inaccessible; no development God does not attend in person and which he cannot penetrate with his grace. We must never think that the very things God abhors he therefore shuns. On the contrary the very thing God abhors he hovers over just because he knows that his presence, his grace, is especially needed there! We are not to thank God for all circumstances, for then we should be thanking him (ridiculously) for evil, wickedness and sin. Yet we must thank him in all circumstances just because he is with us in them all and remains unhandcuffed in them all.

The present iterative imperative means we are to thank God not once, not spasmodically or episodically, but *constantly*. What has ceaseless thanksgiving to do with life? Life blossoms and flourishes for those who are ceaselessly grateful.

The gift-aspect of life

To be ceaselessly grateful means that we recognize the gift-aspect in all of life. Whether it is the food we can't cause to grow or the friends we don't deserve or the serendipities that surprise us or the unwearying patience of God or the ever-effervescing truth of God or the fathomless mercy of God — *it is all gift*. Life is a gift above all else.

It means we recognize a giver whom we can thank, since there can be no gift without a giver.

It means we shall also be the happiest and healthiest — because holiest — people anywhere. People who give thanks to the giver are those who have stopped looking inward; they are lifted above themselves. Let's not deceive ourselves. As psychology is popularized more and more, people gain a smattering of psychological concepts and vocabulary; at the same time they spend more and more time thinking about themselves — with the result that the popularizing of psychology (which is supposed to make the populace feel better) appears to make the populace feel worse. Hypochondria concerning physical aches and pains is bad enough. Add to it a hypochondria of the psyche and people are convinced they aren't well only to render themselves unwell. You understand the progression. To engage in endless navel-gazing is to imagine you have a pain in your tummy. Next you worry about the (imaginary) pain in your tummy until your worrying gives rise to a tummy-disorder. Now you have a real pain in your tummy. When neither the pain nor the anxiety disappears readily the next stage is depression over the syndrome. On it goes. So far from helping the populace much pop-psychology addicts them to themselves. We need to be turned *out of* ourselves. But how?

Here too is a progression. To discern the ceaseless gift-dimension is to be moved to give thanks; to give thanks is to thank someone in particular (namely, the giver himself); therefore to give thanks ceaselessly is to be fixed upon God. End of hypochondria, whether of body, mind or spirit! End of moaning, groaning, griping, whining! Now we are lifted out of ourselves as we look above ourselves to thank God for gifts he has strewn lavishly throughout our lives. The food, the friends, the serendipities, the patience, the ever-effervescing truth and fathomless mercy of God — these so riddle my life that they leap to mind unbidden. What would fall off your tongue in an instant? And in five minutes with a sheet of paper in front of you? In five minutes you would be looking for a second sheet! The happiest and healthiest people are those who resonate with the verb, "Give thanks," in the imperative mood and the present iterative tense. I was serious when I told my questioner that grammar is the key to life.

Worship is adoration

Gratitude renders us holy and therefore profoundly healthy and happy as it turns our gaze away from ourselves and fixes it upon God. This happens in many ways.

The note sounded in Psalm 100 is one heard everywhere in

scripture. "Enter God's gates with thanksgiving and his courts with praise! Give thanks to him, bless his name! For the Lord is good; his steadfast love endures forever, and his faithfulness to all generations." Worship is adoration. What we adore in God is precisely what we are moved to thank him for. Then thank him we shall. In so doing we shall adore him, worship him.

I sag every time I hear the expression, "worship-experience." An ecclesiastical event that begins with a service of worship is evaluated later. Everyone filling in the evaluation-sheet is asked to comment on "the worship-experience." But as soon as we speak of this we plainly have in mind our own experience. At this point worship has been corrupted into something that is supposed to fuel our experience. But it's nothing less than a corruption! Worship is not a technique or tool for elevating us; it is the adoration of God, even as the essence of adoration is thanksgiving.

Not fewer than six times a day do I tell my wife that I love her. I don't tell her repeatedly that I love her because telling her makes me feel good. Neither do I tell her because she is neurotically insecure and if I don't tell her she will unravel or even leave me. I tell her because I cannot thank her enough. She has loved me so lavishly that the love she spills over me splashes back upon her in the form of gratitude. It is love so deep that it uncovers the inconsistencies and contradictions in me without shaming or annihilating me; love so undeflectable that not even my residual sin has induced her to stop loving me.

Nonetheless my dear wife would be the first to admit that she is a spiritually stunted, sin-beset creature whose sinnership warps her, including of course her love for me. Therefore let us instead contemplate God: *his* love for all of us is inexhaustibly deep and eternally undeflectable. Little wonder, then, that we're commanded to enter his gates with thanksgiving and his courts with praise! Because you and I are deformed creatures of dull wit and calcified heart the psalmist knows he has to repeat himself if we're to get the message. Therefore he tells us immediately that God is not only good but also faithful. His nature and purpose are steadfast love.

To grasp this is to be overwhelmed with a gratitude which expresses itself in adoration. Thanksgiving is the essence of worship.

Antidote to coveting

Further, thanksgiving ensures contentment. The uncontented are those who are not grateful just because they are covetous. Covetousness and contentedness are mutually exclusive. To covet is to forfeit contentment; on the other hand, to be contented is to dispel coveting. Martin Luther was correct when he said that to keep the first commandment is to keep them all, while to violate the tenth commandment is to violate them all. The first commandment is that we recognize no other deity than the Holy One of Israel; the tenth, that we covet nothing at all. Honour the first, and we honour them all; violate the last, and we violate them all. It's easy to understand. If we violate the tenth, coveting whatever our neighbour has, including his good reputation, soon we are bearing false witness against him. At this point the ninth commandment is violated. If we covet, we covet our neighbour's goods, and soon we are stealing from him. Now the eighth is violated. If we covet, we covet our neighbour's spouse, and soon we are committing adultery. Now the seventh is violated. As covetousness comes to rage in us we get to the point where we resent everything about our neighbour, and soon we feel murderous toward him. Now the sixth is violated.

Then are we to *will* ourselves not to covet? But coveting comes naturally to fallen people. Given our sin-orientation, fierce determination not to covet will only produce grim frustration and scarcely suppressed fury. Plainly we need a new orientation. It must be gratitude to God for the gifts he continues to give us — regardless of what someone else appears to have! Thankfulness ensures contentment. To give thanks in all circumstances is profoundly to be contented in all circumstances; not to be pleased with all circumstances, not to be complacent in all circumstances, not to be stupidly indifferent to all circumstances, but profoundly to know that there is no area or development in life where the gift-dimension is absent, and therefore there is no day on which the giver himself is not be thanked and our hearts to be rendered content.

Contentment crushes covetousness. Contentment is born of gratitude. Thanksgiving ensures contentment.

Courage for the future

Moreover, thanksgiving signifies our recognition of God's provision in the past and fires our courage for the future. The apostle Paul had wanted to go to Rome for three years. Rome was the capital city of the empire, and he wanted to declare his gospel in the seat of the imperial power. It was also the gateway to western Europe, and Paul's missionary vocation impelled him to push on past Rome into Spain where he could announce the news of Jesus Christ to those who had never heard the name.

Three years had elapsed since he had written the Christians in Rome, informing them of his plans. No doubt he had often wondered if he were ever going to get to Rome and what sort of reception he would find there. After all, many were suspicious of Paul, to say the least. Since his reputation as a fierce Christian-basher was widespread, Christians tended to dismiss their suspicion only upon meeting him face-to-face and spending time with him. The Roman Christians had never met him. How long would it take for them to trust him? Would they ever "warm up" to him? His courage sagged.

In addition there were the sights that greeted Paul as he approached Rome. The huge fleet anchored at Misenum; the holiday beaches at Baiae where pleasure-preoccupied "swingers" splashed around mindlessly; the vast storehouses and granaries and merchant ships at Puteoli. What was he, a diminutive Jewish tentmaker, supposed to do in the face of all this? His courage sagged again.

Then he saw them! A delegation of Christians from Rome! They couldn't wait for him to get to the city, and so had walked miles to meet him. Some had walked as far as the town of Three Taverns, 33 miles from Rome; others had walked to the Forum of Appius, 43 miles! And what a greeting it was! In his write-up of the incident Luke tells us that there was a "meeting." The English word is far too weak. The Greek *apantesis* is the word used when dignitaries go out to greet a king or a general or a victorious hero. The Christians from Rome who had tramped those miles (and would have to tramp them back) were investing Paul with immense honour, esteem and appreciation.

In that instant the apostle's misgivings disappeared. Provision had been made for him. He wasn't met with ice-cold frigidity; he wasn't going to be kept to the fringes of the Christian fellowship in Rome on account of his past persecutions. Luke tells us that when Paul saw the delegation of Roman Christians he "gave thanks and took courage." He gave thanks for provision made in the past, and took courage because he knew that provision would be made for the future.

We give thanks because we're impelled to thank God for his unending goodness to us. As we do, we are lifted out of ourselves, lifted above ourselves, and find that whining, complaining and bellyaching flee.

What's more, our thankfulness will ever be the essence of our worship; it will ever ensure our contentment, dispelling covetousness; and it will ever signify our recognition of God's mercies in the past even as it lends us courage for the future.

Then let us exclaim with the psalmist, "O give thanks to the Lord, for he is good; for his steadfast love endures forever."

Chapter 17

SPIRITUAL "EXPERIENCES": A GOSPEL-CONSEQUENCE OR DANGEROUS DELUSION?

As in the best of marriages, our relationship with God is sustained by commitment.

> *Marriage is sustained by commitment; it's a relationship we're often unaware of, one that has moments of ecstasy as well as quiet contentment. So, too, our relationship with God is an ever-present reality, and not something we should seek in terms of isolated "experiences" that have nothing to do with God.*

We live in an age that craves psychedelic extravaganzas; we crave the most intense experiences. The movie theatre we patronize is the one with quadraphonic sound: the huge speakers, strategically placed, cause us to feel we're at the foot of the mountain when the volcano erupts.

Then there's the IMAX picture screen at Ontario Place. To see the movie of the stunt flier is to feel you're a stunt flier yourself. (Also to learn that the movie is best not seen on a full stomach!)

We must not overlook the proliferation of sex manuals. Sex is now a high-skill performance ostensibly issuing in a high-intensity experience.

And then I hear the preacher say to young people, "Don't get high on drugs; get high on Jesus." I wince. Is not Jesus demeaned (to say the least) by speaking of him as a non-criminal substitute for a chemical hit?

People tell me they've never had a "religious experience." Do they know what they're looking for? How would a religious experience differ from a psychological or human one? Many such people flit from church to church, sect to sect, guru to guru, pursuing the ever-elusive religious experience.

Nonetheless, I understand the divinely-placed longing for the transcendent which underlies their request. We are made for God. Because we do not know God we're aware of an emptiness, even though we cannot identify what is missing. A secularized world in fact cannot identify it as spiritual emptiness, but even a secularized world has an emptiness amounting to a vacuum.

A vacuum, everyone knows, does not remain if there's anything ready-to-hand that can fill it, even clutter it. Paul insists God has created humankind with a longing for him. Yet humankind is fallen. In the wake of the fall and the human distortion arising from it the longing for God is not recognized for what it is. As a result the vacuum gets cluttered with debris. The bottom line is a hunger that is always being fed with substitutes that are less than God.

My question to those on a quest is this: Do you want religious experiences (so-called), or do you want *God*, the holy one of Israel? Do you want a psychological "light-up," or do you want to be known by and know, be embraced by and embrace the one who is indeed the creator, rescuer and sustainer of the cosmos and of your own existence?

In scripture the commonest metaphor for faith is marriage. I can ask myself, do I want to be married or do I want an experience? I want to be married; I want the state of being married. Insofar as I *am* married, then certain experiences will follow naturally. But if I start by pursuing an experience that seems to be something like that of those who are married, then achieving this or that experience will never confer the actuality of marriage. At best I shall be left with an "as if married" experience. But "as if married" means "not married at all." Therefore, whatever my experience might be, it could never be one of being married.

An age-old quest

The quest for religious experience is not new at all; in fact it's as old as humankind. Think of Mexican peasants eating peyote beans. The beans give them a drug-induced "high" to which they attach religious significance. Or consider the techniques used to get people into trances. You follow a formula and repeat a sound self-hypnotically until you move into unusual mental space.

Even in the days of our Lord's earthly ministry there were devotees of Greek mystery religions. One such religion had a practice its disciples swore by. The devotee stood in a pit covered by a latticework grill. A bull was led onto the grill, where its throat was slashed. Blood poured through the grill onto the devotee. She was then pronounced "reborn for eternity." Was she? Or was this exercise a clutter-substitute for that renewal at God's hand in virtue of the sacrifice of his Son? It should be obvious by now that the quest for "spiritual experience" is fraught with danger. After all, cults, not to mention the occult, are contemporary equivalents to the latticework and the bull's blood. If we're to speak of "spiritual experience" we should understand that *not all the spirits are holy*. Scripture says as much as it does about spiritual conflict just because it recognizes this. And even where spirits are not especially unholy they may yet be decidedly unhelpful.

Frankly, to seek spiritual experiences is to be looking in the wrong direction. The prophet Isaiah cries, "Seek ye the *Lord* . . ." Nowhere are we urged to pursue experiences. We are to seek that God whom we can seek at all only because he has first sought us and found us in Christ Jesus his Son.

Sustained by commitment

Consider again the analogy of marriage. To be married is to live in a relationship. The relationship *is* the reality of marriage. Within this relationship a great variety of experiences come and go. There is also the "experience" of not being conscious of anything marital at all. I remain married when I'm in my study writing, even though I'm not conscious of being married. There is also the experience of quiet contentment in the presence of my wife. Then there is a more intense excitement as we share something extraordinary together. And of course there are moments of ecstasy. But no marriage is *sustained* by ecstasy. You can't be ecstatic 24 hours per day. Marriages are sustained by commitment.

Further, when two lives are fused together the suffering of one becomes the suffering of both. If one suffers and the other refuses to have anything to do with that suffering or to make any accommodation at all, then that marriage is listing and in danger of sinking.

The truth of the matter is that 90 percent of the time being married is to be unaware of any particular experience at all. When I see my wife at the supper table the "experience" I have (if it can be called that) is simply that I am glad to see her. But this is scarcely extraordinary. For most of the time to be married is to live in each other's presence without experiencing anything unusual, whether positive or negative. If you were constantly taking the temperature of your marriage by asking yourself, "What kind of experience am I having at this moment?" you would soon have no marriage at all; and soon you would not be sane.

This "90 percent of the time" doesn't mean nothing is going on at such moments; the *relationship* is going on; it's always going on, and the relationship is everything.

So it is with that relationship with God we call faith. Everything is going on at all times regardless of how we feel. Nonetheless I should never deny that we do feel. There are in fact moments of heightened awareness, greater intensity, and occasionally, moments of inexpressible ecstasy — as well as moments of piercing pain.

On the day of Pentecost Peter, spokesperson for the apostles, was preaching the truth and reality of Jesus Christ, crucified, raised, now ruling. Peter acquainted his hearers with him who is the sinner's judge and only saviour, and therefore the sinner's only hope. Luke tells us that as all of this struck home they were "cut to the heart" and cried, "What are we going to do?" They felt as though they had been stabbed in a surprise attack. Sudden, stabbing conviction of sinnership doesn't come to everyone with this intensity. But whenever it does I should never pretend it isn't genuine spiritual experience. Any experience that impels people to embrace Jesus Christ is *of God*.

So far from describing piercing pain, Paul told the Christians in Corinth that on one occasion he was "caught up into paradise," where he "heard things that cannot be uttered." The experience was so unusual, so intensely pleasurable, that he didn't have adequate words for it. In my reading of Christian biography I have come upon several similar incidents. I have no reason to doubt their veracity.

At the same time, Paul never urges people to pursue the ecstatic experience he had. He never tells them to try to work it up or put themselves in the mood for it. Worked-up artificiality would guarantee that it wasn't an experience of God. Instead he immediately tells the congregation in Corinth of another experience of his that he *does* want them to have: in the midst of chronic discomfort and weakness to know that God's grace would ever be sufficient, just as God's strength would ever be made perfect not in our strength but in our weakness. This is what he wanted them to know and find validated in their lives one hundred times over.

Freezing the moment

We find the same thing when Peter, James and John were with Jesus on the mount of transfiguration. The three disciples were given a vision of Moses and Elijah (the two greatest figures in Israel); they were also made privy to that Word that insists Jesus is greater than Moses and Elijah inasmuch as Jesus alone is the Son of God. It was an ecstatic experience and they wanted to freeze the moment, build a shrine, consecrate the spot then and there, relive the experience over and over. Jesus, however, didn't let them do any of this. He took the three down the mountainside to a village where an epileptic boy was convulsing, parents were distraught, the disciples appeared helpless and religious leaders were agitating a crowd. Jesus told the three men that the experience on the mountain was good; of course it was good, since it was God-given and they were meant to have it. Still, among the convulsing and the agitated was where they belonged.

Then there are experiences so quiet and undramatic as to be virtually the constant background to our lives. Jesus says, "My sheep hear my voice; I know them, and they follow me." Needless to say Jesus doesn't mean we're constantly "hearing things," as though we were undergoing auditory hallucinations. He means his people are unremittingly possessed of the conviction that he is the one to be followed. They continue to hear his voice inasmuch as they're never without the conviction that he is the good shepherd and ever will be. It's not a startling or ecstatic experience. But it is the foundation on which the life of any Christian is built. "My sheep keep on hearing my voice; I continue to know them, and they keep on following me."

Second nature

Surely most of our Christian experience is of the non-startling, non-ecstatic order. Most of it is so very ordinary that it becomes second nature to us; in truth it *is* our new nature. Paul writes to the Christians in Colosse, "God has delivered us from the dominion of darkness and transferred us to the kingdom of his beloved son, in whom we have redemption, the forgiveness of sins." There is nothing dramatic about this. While a few people can certainly point to a datable, never-to-be-forgotten moment when they were delivered, most cannot. All that matters is this: as we read newspapers, listen to newscasts, observe social trends and ponder all that tends to confuse, beguile and humanly impoverish people, we know in our hearts that we *have* been delivered from the dominion of darkness and have been transferred to the kingdom of Jesus Christ; in him we know ourselves to be forgiven people. This too is experience; elemental experience.

There is one experience, genuinely of God, that *all* Christians are to own without exception. Just as marriage fuses together the joys and suffering of two people, by faith you and I are fused to Jesus Christ — and this makes cross-bearing inevitable. The analogy breaks down here. Although fused to our Lord we are never called to bear his cross (only he can do that); but in his company we are most certainly called to bear *our* cross. Our discipleship requires a sacrifice we readily make for our Lord's sake.

It is not "spiritual experiences" that we need; it is *God himself.* To be rightly related to him is to be acquainted with what St. Peter calls the "many-splendoured grace of God." What steals over us when we neither look for it nor cultivate it will be richer than anything we have anticipated; rich enough indeed to satisfy us until the day when faith gives way to sight and we know even as we are now known.

Chapter 18

OUR SECRET STRENGTH

To be content is to possess unfailing strength.

Ambition and wealth tend to distract and preoccupy, whereas godly contentment keeps us steadfast even when fortune smiles more broadly on others. Contentment keeps our human relationships strong, is a qualification for leadership in the church, and reflects the self-giving lordship of Jesus himself.

Who is the strongest person in the world? Physically, the one who can lift 650 pounds; constitutionally, he who does not succumb to disease; psychologically, she who cannot be "bent" through brainwashing. But who is the strongest personally or spiritually? Here we may be surprised. The Greek word that means to be possessed of unfailing strength is translated as "contented." To be contented, profoundly so, is to possess a strength adequate in the face of every blow, threat or temptation. Contentment is strength.

Contentment is not indifference, found typically among the lazy or the callous. There is no virtue here. Neither is it the same as apathy, found in people who have given up on life; nor is it the same as inertia, found most commonly in people who are depressed.

In his letter to the congregation in Philippi, St. Paul insists he has learned to be content in any situation. No one, not even his worst enemy, ever accused Paul of being lazy or a quitter. Such profound contentment, however, was learned. He didn't always have it. In his writings he drops hints here and there as to how he acquired it. The most sparkling is the little verse, "For me, to live is Christ." Or, "Christ means life for me." It sounds so simple, yet points to so much that words could never capture.

It's as though you hear music that moves you profoundly. You attempt to speak of the event to someone else. You fumble and stumble, recognizing that what you're saying sounds simple-minded or childish in view of the deepest depths it is supposed to elucidate. Finally you give up, realizing that if your friend's heart is moved as yours is, words are superfluous. And if your friend's heart is not moved as yours is, words are useless.

So it is with our experience of our Lord Jesus Christ. If your heart resonates with mine, you know the words we use to speak of our common experience are as feeble as the words of a newspaper reporter describing Itzak Perlman's violin. In any case, if your heartbeat quickens when you hear Paul say, "For me to live is Christ . . . I have learned in whatever situation I am to be content," then you will also know how and why and where he has learned to be content.

There is a deep heart-hunger. It's not grief; no one has died. It's not misery; there's no reason to be miserable. It's not depression; no need to call in physician or psychiatrist. Concerning this heart-hunger Augustine insisted we are made for God; we are never going to be contented — profoundly — until we come to terms with this fact.

Contentment arises when we recognize the face of God shining upon us in the face of Jesus. It arises through our intimacy with him. And this intimacy, like intimacy elsewhere, we do not cheapen through careless prattle.

Where godliness flourishes

Contentment is the atmosphere in which faith thrives and character flourishes. Faith and character add up to godliness. "There is great gain in godliness with contentment," writes the apostle, "for we brought nothing into the world, and we cannot take anything out of the world; but if we have food and clothing, with these we shall be content." I have spoken several times at the Scarborough Christian Teacher's Association. One fellow I came to know well, a high school science teacher and a Mennonite, I recently met up with after not seeing him for some time.

"How's it going?" I asked, expecting nothing more than a shorthand greeting. Instead he began to blurt, as pitiable as a child lost in a department store. A few years ago he had decided to speculate in real estate. He made money at it. Speculated some more. Made more money. Speculated some more. Lost it all suddenly? No, he made an even bigger bundle. It became an all-consuming preoccupation with him. He had lost his Mennonite simplicity and the Christian profundity that goes with it. And with this loss he had also lost every last shred of contentment. "My head is all messed up," he told me, "and my heart I can't even recognize." Then we had to depart. Do you know what he will do next? He will leave his wife. Am I being uncharitable? Ask me how many couples I have seen blown apart when their newfound fortune preoccupied them.

There is an ambition that is entirely appropriate. We encourage it, especially in our youth. People should be eager to develop and use their talents, to do work that stretches their abilities. There is another kind of ambition, however, that scares me. This kind is a conscienceless climb to the top, driven by a desire to gain wealth or fame, to be a showboat, to dominate others or to strut. I've found we have far more to fear from the ambitious person than from the nasty person. Because the nasty person is always nasty we can step around her. We know what to expect and we can take evasive action. The crudely ambition person, however, manipulates, schemes, lies. He will smile sweetly at the same time as he is plotting how he's going to step on you in order to step up the ladder himself. And if the ambitious person is also insecure (as most ambitious people are) he will lash out like a cornered animal however little he thinks he is threatened. No one can step around this fellow. He chews up people. They are mere fodder for him.

"There is great gain in godliness with contentment. For we

brought nothing into the world, and we can take nothing out; but if we have food and clothing, with these we shall be content." Contentment is the atmosphere — the only atmosphere — in which faith thrives and character flourishes.

Where relationships prosper

Contentment is essential if our human relationships are to prosper and be for us and others our richest support and nourishment. Three thousand years ago in Israel a young man decided it was time he ventured forth into the wider world. He left his village thinking he would make a home for himself wherever he found people hospitable. He came upon Micah, who asked where he was going.

"Nowhere in particular, just wherever I feel myself one with the neighbours."

"Why don't you stay with me," said Micah. The young man did. We're told he was content to stay with Micah and became "like one of Micah's own sons." In other words, the family adopted him. A bond was forged that was as strong as the bond of birth.

Several hundred years earlier Moses was fleeing for his life when he came upon seven foreign women, Midianites, who were struggling to care for sheep. He helped them. They told their father Reuel, who invited Moses for dinner, a most significant gesture in those days. We are told Moses was content to dwell with the man. The father gave Moses one of his seven daughters, Zipporah, as wife. Their first child they named Gershom (*Ger* is Hebrew for sojourner) because, said Moses, "I have become a sojourner in a foreign land."

There is a sense in which we all feel ourselves sojourners in a foreign land, especially if we are Christians. Then it is all the more important we forge the strongest, profoundest bonds with other people and fellow-disciples. These bonds can be forged only as we are content.

I have seen dozens of friendships dry up and blow away as someone ceased to be content. Here's what happens. Two people genuinely sustain and nurture each other in real friendship *until* one of them has better luck in life. A higher-paying job, a gifted child, an unforeseen inheritance, greater social prominence. The other becomes slightly jealous, only slightly at first, but then resentful, soon critical and finally hostile. At this point the friendship is spiraling down — fast — and soon it won't sustain or nurture anyone. The downward spiral can be stopped before it even begins by one thing: contentment. If we are genuinely content, profoundly so, someone else's greater good fortune doesn't do nasty things in us.

The young man from the village as well as Moses fleeing out of Egypt found themselves in enduring human relationships that sustained and nurtured them even though they were sojourners in a strange land. As sojourners all of us are going to find ourselves treasured and nourished and therefore enriched only as we are profoundly content and consequently do not become jealous and resentful, critical and hostile. It is contentment that holds us in human relationships that are unfailingly strong.

Where leadership thrives

Contentment is a qualification for leadership in the church. Leaders are not to be greedy, says the apostle, for *anything*, whether fame, recognition, or money. I understand why contentment is a qualification for leadership in the church. The person who lacks it will always use his position to feed his greed, ambition and self-advertisement.

Leadership in the church must always reflect the lordship Jesus Christ himself exercises over us. He is named Lord and is to be honoured as such for one reason only: he has been to hell and back for us. In his earthly ministry Jesus spoke of bigshots who don't do this; instead, they "lord" it over others by browbeating them, twisting arms, pouting petulantly. Those who like to inflate themselves larger than everyone else, says Jesus, are those who like to be a big toad in a small pond. But the only genuine leader is the one who can call followers to a discipleship of self-renunciation; and the only person who does this is the person who has shouldered a cross first himself. In the church of Jesus Christ contentment will always be a qualification for leadership.

How important is it then? How essential that we learn to be

content in whatever situation? Pretend for a minute that we're not content. The apostle Jude has some startling things to say about us: malcontents are found in the company of grumblers, loudmouthed boasters, self-serving flatterers, leering lusters (Jude 16).

Let's think positively. To be content is to be possessed of unfailing strength, according to scripture.

Here faith thrives and character flourishes. Human relationships are forged that last. And leadership in the church reflects the self-giving lordship of Jesus himself.

SPRING

The Wonder of God's Love

As we understand and soak ourselves in
Christ's love and compassion,
we extend that love to all of life's relationships.

Chapter 19

WHAT MATTERS ABOVE ALL ELSE

*The measure of our love of God is whether we
love him without measure.*

---

*The first commandment
shouldn't be blended into
the second. We are to love
God supremely, then our
neighbour as ourselves.
His love then begets in
us an upward spiral of
gratitude, humility, and
especially love of fellow-
believers. Yet all this
is a foretaste of what
awaits us in glory.*

I have never had a stroke, as far as I know. One aftermath of some strokes is that the sufferer cannot say what he wants to say. Those attending him can only guess and guess again.

As a minister sometimes I feel — stroke-like — that I too am not articulating what I long to communicate, and therefore people are left guessing.

One guess is that I'm trying to improve the moral tone of the community. To be sure, I should be only happy if it were improved. I am scarcely a booster of immorality or amorality. Nevertheless, at the end of the day I am not a moralist, concerned with having the community conform to a code. I am a minister of the gospel of Jesus Christ.

Another guess is that I am concerned to have religious observances better attended. To be sure, I should like this; it bothers me that our church-rolls carry so many people who are never seen at worship. At the same time, Jesus himself reminds us that the way is straight, the gate is narrow, and the few who enter upon it and persist in it are few indeed.

Another guess (chiefly by those without church-connection) is that I am in the business of providing an affordable counselling service. Of course I am glad to offer whatever help I can to any suffering human being.

But, at bottom, what am I really trying to do? At the risk of speaking like the stroke-sufferer, I shall make another attempt: *I am trying to facilitate and foster love for God.* You see, I have never lost sight of the "great commandment" reinforced by Jesus himself. When asked, "Which commandment is first of all?" he replied, "Hear O Israel, the Lord our God, the Lord is one; and you shall love the Lord your God with all your heart, with all your soul, with all your mind, and with all your strength. The second is this: You shall love your neighbour as yourself." These two are never to be separated. At the same time, the first cannot be reduced to the second or collapsed into the second. It is not the case that by loving the neighbour we also love God. God insists on being loved for himself, being loved as God. The first command ever remains the first: we are to love God.

In truth, we're not exactly commanded to "love God" but to "love *the Lord* our God." The difference is crucial. "The Lord," Yahweh, is the proper name of God everywhere in the Bible. The Hebrew word is spelled with no vowels. A word with no vowels cannot be pronounced and therefore cannot be translated; neither can there be a substitute for it. Yahweh cannot be translated into Zeus (the deity of the ancient Greeks), or into Gitchi Manitou (the deity of Amerindians), or into Sophia (radical feminists' impersonation of God) or into Supreme Being (the deity of modernity). Neither can it be translated into any of the gods people worship all the time: the American way of life, Canadian nationalism, or even something as crude as undisguised mammon. Neither can Yahweh be translated into the highest cultural achievement (however rich) or the profoundest environmentalism (however necessary). The name of God admits no rivals, approximations or substitutions. We are not to love God-in-general; we are to love "the Lord" our God.

He alone is creator; he fashioned a people to be a light to the nations; he spoke with Moses and seared upon him what the world will never be without; he arrested and infused prophets; and he, ultimately, became incarnate in Jesus of Nazareth. Yahweh alone is God and he cannot be co-opted by anyone or anything.

Why should we love God?

What prompts us to love God? Surely our gratitude compels our love for him. He has made us and ever sustains us. This is reason enough. Yet this is not where the Hebrew mind begins. It begins not with creation but with redemption: God has saved us. The Hebrew heart is always moved most profoundly in reflecting upon our rescue at God's hand.

Think of the Ten Commandments. They're not an abstract moral code; neither do they enjoin conformity to a code. The Commandments describe the shape, pattern, direction and freedom of the life of that man or woman who knows God has rescued him or her and is everlastingly grateful to God. The preface to the Commandments is crucial: "I am the Lord your God who brought you out of the land of Egypt, out of the house of bondage." Deliverance! Rescue! This is what leaves us breathless! If we know in our hearts that God has delivered us from anything at all, rescued us in any respect, then our gratitude will render us eager to have our lives take on the shape, pattern, direction which our rescuer wills for us. One aspect of this pattern (in fact *the* aspect that governs all others) is that we love him. We shall love God ardently inasmuch as our gratitude to him dissolves all hesitation or reservation.

An answering love

Yet we love God for another reason: God's love for us creates in us and elicits from us our answering love for him. I love my children. I am overjoyed to find them loving me. I like to think that I could continue to love them even if they never loved me, even if they answered my love with Arctic iciness. But how difficult it would be, because what a heartbreak! I want my love for them to create in them and elicit from them a love for me, which would then magnify my love for them, which would in turn swell their love for me as the spiral of love became more intense and more wonderful. This is how God loves! His love remains undiminished even though there are countless hearts that remain cold and stony. What such people have not yet grasped is that they were *made for love*. They were made to love God. They would be most authentically and nobly human if only they surrendered their indifference or defiance. Then they would find that God's great love had begun to create in them and elicit from them a love for God through which they became most truly themselves.

Selfish-fulfillment

Obviously I am speaking here of human self-fulfillment. We have to be careful here, since what passes for self-fulfillment in our era is, at bottom, selfish-fulfillment. When people complain they are not fulfilled they usually mean they can't get what they want. Seminars provide techniques for "self-fulfillment," giving people tools whereby they can finally get what they want. What's more, since I am a fallen creature and therefore sin-riddled, fulfillment of my sinful self could only result in a monstrosity better left unimagined! (Secularites who prattle glibly about self-fulfillment never seem to grasp this point or understand that fulfillment of the depraved self results in intensified depravity!) At a much profounder level, however, to love God *is* the true fulfillment of my self, since to love God is to know the remedy for my sinful self.

The psalmist is correct when he writes, "My soul thirsts for God . . . my heart and flesh cry out for the living God." To have our thirst and outcry met is surely to be most profoundly fulfilled. It should not surprise us, then, that we're most profoundly ourselves when we most self-forgetfully love God. After all, we were made "in the image and likeness" of God, and God, John says so very pithily, *is* love. We have been made *by* love *for* love.

The answer to the question, "Why ought we to love God?" has been rather long. But the length of the answer is nothing compared to the depth of the reality: we are to love God inasmuch as the God

who is love has created and rescued us. In addition, he has fashioned us in such a way that we can become what we are created to
be only by giving ourselves up to him and loving him with an
ardour that reflects the ardour of his love for us. Paradoxically, it is
as we love the God who is not an extension of ourselves that we
most profoundly become ourselves.

A total love

"How ought we to love?" The answer is stated in our text: with all
our heart, soul, mind and strength. Fancy (or fanciful) preachers
finesse the four words, "heart," "soul," "mind," "strength" and
develop a four-point sermon. The truth is, there aren't four points
here; there is only one. In the Hebrew all four words are synony-
mous! When Jesus insisted we are to love God with heart, soul,
mind and strength he was increasing the intensity until we understood that we're to love God totally, with everything in us, without
hesitation, reservation, qualification or calculation. Our love for
God is to be whole-souled, admitting no rivals.

To say we're to love God with all that we have and are is not to
say we're to love nothing else and no one else. There is much else
we are to love: our neighbour, to say the least, also children, parents, spouse. *We are to love much else, yet love nothing else pre-
eminently.* Our love for God must come first.

We've noted that the commonest metaphor for faith, in scripture,
is marriage. Everyone knows (or should know) that exclusivity is
of the essence of marriage, regardless of our society's preoccupation with inclusivity. The relationship we have with our spouse
we're to have with no other man or woman. My wife occupies a
place in my heart and life no one else can occupy. But this is not to
say others have no place in my heart and life. They do! It's just
that the place others occupy (and occupy even at my wife's urging),
cannot encroach upon the place she holds.

Forsaking all others

The older marriage vows contained the line, "and forsaking all others." This didn't mean newly-married couples forsook everyone else, dismissing friends, relatives, needy human beings, henceforth to live in a shriveled, miserable universe of two. It meant they forsook having the kind of relationship with others they now had with each other. Exclusivity is of the essence of marriage. Where this truth is doubted the marriage is destroyed.

If you understand this then you comprehend what prophet and apostle meant when they said God is jealous. This is not to say God is insecure or suspicious, like the husband who rages if he sees his wife talking to another man at a social function. To say God is jealous is simply to acknowledge that exclusivity is of the essence of our love for God.

Our Israelite foreparents in faith, always earthy in their expression of spiritual truth, used to say, "Israel has gone a-whoring after false gods!" They meant the Israelite people had given to other things the whole-souled love they owed God alone. In so doing they had violated their covenant-promise to God, had become unfaithful; and like anyone who "goes a-whoring" had debased themselves.

If we become most profoundly ourselves through loving God, then we debase and denature ourselves through deflecting our first love from God to something else, anything else. God is a jealous God, we're told again and again. He insists that he be acknowledged as **God**. If we refuse to acknowledge the exclusivity of our relationship with him, we destroy the relationship.

Results of loving God

What is the outcome of our love for God? One result we've already seen: insofar as we answer with love the love that has made us and redeemed us we become most truly ourselves.

Another is that we love our fellow-believers who, like us, aspire to love God without hesitation or reservation. In his first epistle John writes, "Everyone who believes Jesus is the Christ is a child of God; and everyone who loves the parent loves the child." We are to love our neighbour (any suffering human being); but we're especially to love fellow-believers, fellow-lovers of God.

In 1663 one of England's finest puritan writers, Thomas Watson, wrote a little book, *A Divine Cordial*. It was meant to be a tonic for Christians who had become dispirited through savage persecution in Britain. In it Watson laid down **14** (!) "tests of love to God." One such test was love for fellow-Christians. "Like a fair face with a scar" is how Watson described a fellow Christian. "You who cannot love another because of his infirmities, how would you have God love you?" I emphasize the matter of loving fellow-Christians because I know discouragement abounds in the Christian life, difficulties permeate church life, dispiritedness alights on us like the 'flu, isolation blows its chill breath upon us, and before we know what has happened someone else has dropped away from the congregation. One test of our love to God, says Watson, is that we love those who love God.

Another result is that we rejoice to see God's name glorified and his truth exalted. One afternoon a parishioner came to see me and told me she would do anything to help me in my work, anything she could to free me for my work because, she said, what issues from the Streetsville pulpit honours God. Of this much I am certain: through the service she renders that woman herself honours God every bit as much. Myself, I rejoice to see and hear God glorified, the gospel commended, his truth enhanced, love owned, mercy confessed, faithfulness welcomed, and his people cherished.

A further result is that we, God's people, are humbled. One day I overheard a conversation between a friend of mine and another woman. The second woman mentioned she'd been asked to render some service in the church, then added that she regarded it beneath her. "I'm not that small," she said in conclusion. My friend quietly replied, "What you really mean is, you aren't that big; you aren't big enough." God's love, poured upon us, never demeans or shrivels us. God's love dignifies us and renders us big. So big, in fact, that no service to him and his people will ever be found too small. Our love for God humbles us without humiliating us. We are only loving him whose love for us washed feet and endured contempt.

The final result of our love for God is that it will be consummated by what God has prepared for all who love him. Paul insists that what God has prepared for all who love him cannot be described or imagined, so glorious is it. Our love for God will be crowned so gloriously as to leave us speechless yet forever adoring. Nonetheless, the love he has already shed abroad in our hearts is surely a clue to it. Then for the full splendour of what he has prepared for us we can wait confidently now, just because we have already tasted and enjoyed that love that has quickened ours.

Then we shall continue to love him. We know why we are to love him; we know how. Do we know *how much*? Let Bernard of Clairvaux, a mediaeval thinker and hymnwriter, have the last word: "The measure of our love to God is to love him without measure."

Chapter 20

WITH EVERY PASSION BLENDING

We are to embody the whole range of God's passion.

To say God is impassioned doesn't mean he is emotionally unstable, erratic or easily manipulated. On the contrary, God displays jealousy, anger, joy, mercy — but always as an expression of his love. Our response to him must be identical.

"We passed you on the street, Victor, and you didn't even see us. You must have been living in your head — again." Many people have said this to me many times. I can only conclude that I appear to live in my head. Still, I don't live in my head exclusively!

I live in my body as well. When people tell me I must have been a vicious Neanderthal to have been a boxer I always let them know I have never enjoyed being hurt and have never enjoyed hurting others. What I liked about my boxing days was the training. The sheer bodiliness of it. When I was able to run I ran not because I thought I was extending my life by ten minutes; I ran through the streets of Streetsville for one reason: I found immense bodily pleasure in running.

Yet not only do I live in my head and my body, I live in my heart as well. I live in my passions. I've never been ashamed of being an impassioned person. For this reason my favourite hymn-line, from "Lead us, heavenly Father, lead us," is "Love with every passion blending." This line states that love (speaking here of human love) is foundational. All other passions must be subordinated to and blended with the grand passion of love.

God is impassioned

But we human beings are not the only persons who love. God loves too. God is impassioned.

The church hasn't always admitted this. In fact, for centuries the mediaeval church upheld the doctrine of the impassability of God, stating that God is wholly devoid of passion. Now, I know why the church thought it had to uphold this doctrine, yet I also know what was lost when God was said to be without passion.

The church felt it had to say this because to say God is impassioned meant two things: God is emotionally unstable or erratic, and he can be manipulated emotionally. All of us know how difficult it is to live with someone who is emotionally unstable or erratic, and how inappropriate it is to be manipulated. It was felt that since God is neither unstable nor capable of being manipulated, God had to be pronounced as wholly without passion.

But when the church declared this, the living person of God was lost; which is to say, God himself was lost. Our mediaeval Christian foreparents inevitably had to say God does not suffer; God *cannot* suffer. Of what help to suffering people like you and me is a God who knows nothing of suffering himself? Inevitably our mediaeval foreparents, denying the passion of God, rendered God an icicle, numb. What could a God devoid of anguish say or do for us when we are anguish-riddled every day? Inevitably our foreparents rendered God a non-person. Then what relationship could there be between people who are persons and a God who is a non-person? No relationship at all.

They were correct in maintaining that God is not unstable and cannot be manipulated. But they were wrong in holding that God is devoid of passion. Scripture speaks everywhere of the passion of God, just because scripture speaks everywhere of the person of God.

Consider just four aspects of the passion of God: his love, jealousy, anger and joy.

God is love

Love is God's essence, his innermost character. His jealousy, anger and grief, on the other hand, are all reactions in him to something about us (specifically, to our sin). But God's love isn't a *reaction* in God at all; it is what he *is* eternally. God's love is what he would be eternally even if the creation had never appeared. The apostle John writes, "God *is* love." To be sure, God hates, rages, grieves. But nowhere are we told that God *is* hatred, rage or grief. These are reactions within the heart of that God whose eternal nature is constant, persistent, undeflectable love.

When prophets and apostles tell us God is love, however, they are quick to tell us as well what love is not. Love is not indulgence. God indulges no one and nothing. In the same way God tolerates nothing. (We must always be sure to understand that God never tolerates sin; God *forgives* sin.) Neither is love sentimental froth. God is oceans deeper than this.

God's way with Israel as well as his way at the cross make plain that God's love is God's self-giving without qualification. God holds nothing of himself back; his entire self is poured out — without reserve — upon you and me.

When you and I love a little bit we give a little bit of ourselves to someone else and risk a little bit of rejection. As we love more we give more of ourselves and risk greater rejection. To love still more is to give and risk still more. But do you and I ever love anyone so much as to abandon *all* self-protection, throw away *all* the subtle defenses we have spent years perfecting, and risk uttermost rejection? Prophet and apostle insist God has done this not once only in giving up his Son; he does this without letup, since love is his nature.

There is even more to God's love than that self-giving whose vulnerability leaves him defenseless. There is also a humiliation that leaves him with no face to save. Let us never forget that Rome crucified its victims naked. All Christian art depicts Jesus clad in his loincloth on Good Friday. The Roman soldiers may have snatched away his cloak, we are told, but at least they had the decency to leave him his underpants. No, they didn't. One of the cruelest aspects of punishment was public humiliation, especially where Jews were concerned. On the one hand, the Israelite people were body-affirming, completely non-neurotic about body-parts and body-functions; they were earthy. At the same time, they were always modest. In fact they were earthy and modest in equal measure, a distinguishing feature of Israelite consciousness. Forced immodesty was much harder for Jews to endure than for Greeks. Jesus was stripped of minimal modesty for the sake of maximal humiliation.

The humiliation the Father knew in the humiliation of the Son he had known for centuries in the infidelity and waywardness of his people. Centuries before Good Friday the prophet Hosea learned about that humiliation God's love brings upon God, through the humiliation his love for his wife brought him. As earlier related, Hosea's wife, Gomer, traipsed off to the marketplace and sold herself. Pregnancy, of course, is an occupational hazard of prostitution, and Gomer bore three children who were not Hosea's. When Gomer was sufficiently used up that her market-value was all but eroded and she thought she might as well return home (at least she would be fed there) Hosea went down to the marketplace, endured the taunts and crude jokes of the boors and ruffians who lounged around there, and paid 15 shekels to get his wife out of their clutches. Fifteen shekels was half the price of a slave! Why did Hosea endure such humiliation? Because he loved his wife regardless of the cost to himself, regardless of the face that could not be saved. Thereafter Hosea preached about a divine love which loves to the point of public humiliation.

I glory in God's love for me. I know God loves me not in the sense that he feels somewhat warm towards me and thinks about me now and then. God loves me inasmuch as he has poured out himself upon me without qualification; he has risked himself in a vulnerability so drastic as to leave him defenseless; he has undergone a public humiliation without concern to save face or preserve dignity — and all of this in order that my defiant, ungrateful, rebellious, hard heart might be overwhelmed and broken and I throw myself into his arms. This is what it means to say God loves us, and to say God loves us on the grounds that God *is* love, eternally.

God is jealous

"Love with every passion blending," says the hymnwriter. He is speaking of our love, but his line is true of God's love too. But what about the passion of jealousy?

Jealousy in men and women is always a sign of insecurity. A fellow sees his wife dancing at a wedding reception with a guest he has never met before. Immediately he thinks ill of it, and before the one piece of music has stopped he has imagined his wife and this guest in all manner of luridness. A woman groundlessly suspects her husband at the office and mobilizes amateur or professional surveillance in order to expose the bounder who in fact has never turned his head from the computer screen. The more insecure we are, the more ridiculous our jealousy becomes.

But God is not insecure at all. Then whatever we mean by God's jealousy we cannot be speaking of ridiculous suspicion born of pathetic insecurity. To speak of God's jealousy is not to speak of a character-defect in God. God's jealousy is simply God's insistence that he alone be acknowledged, honoured and trusted as God. His jealousy is reflected in the first of the Ten Commandments: "You shall have no other gods before me." God forbids us to worship, adore, or finally entrust with our very selves anyone or anything except him. But he insists on this not because he is a self-important tyrant who has to be flattered. He insists on it for our sakes and *for our blessing.* God knows that if you and I do not honour, love, obey and trust him, we only bring dissolution upon ourselves. To say God is jealous is to say he wants passionately that we honour him, and wants this passionately so that we may always live within the sphere of his blessing. Through the prophet Ezekiel God cries, "I will . . . have mercy upon the whole house of Israel, and I will be jealous for my holy name." As long as Israel honours God in God's claim upon Israel's loyalty, Israel will live within the sphere of God's mercy. To live anywhere else is to bring down dissolution. Because God is "for us," in the words of the psalmist, his jealousy for his own name can only mean God wants passionately to prosper us.

Go back to the first commandment: "You shall have no other

gods before me." This isn't the petulant scolding of the self-inflated. The command is actually a promise: "In the future you won't have to have other gods. In the future I shall prove myself God-enough for you. You will find me, the Holy One of Israel, sufficient for your needs; you won't have to run after any other deities or isms or institutions. Where you are going to live, in the future, I shall be your satisfaction. If my love has delivered you from slavery in Egypt already, isn't my love going to keep you too? — even keep you in whatever wildernesses you find yourselves from time to time? There is no need to look to any other deity and therein forfeit your blessing at my hand."

To say God is jealous is to say he insists on being acknowledged uniquely, exclusively, as God. And since God is "for us," he insists on this acknowledgment *for our own good.* To say God is jealous is to say that fathomless love always warns foolish people against giving their heart away to what isn't fathomless love.

God is angry

Because we are foolish people we do exactly what we're warned not to do. All of us do this, without exception. God reacts to our foolishness in anger or wrath. When God's loving warning goes unheeded, his anger heats up.

While his anger is real (not merely seeming anger, but real anger), it is nevertheless an expression of his love. It has to be, since God *is* love — with every other passion blended into this love. God's anger is never a childish loss of temper or mean-spirited vindictiveness; his anger is never frustrated love now-turned-nasty. God's anger is simply his love burning hot. His anger is his love jarring us awake, shaking us up until we admit that something about us is dreadfully out of order.

Fathomless love aches to see foolish people disdain such love, because the God who is love knows that when humankind disdains him it brings dissolution upon itself. This dissolution is personal, social, institutional, national, international — all of these, all at once. The prophets are quick to supply us with the details: the exploitation of the economically voiceless, the installation of self-serving political rulers, the appearance of a corrupt judicial system. The apostle Paul, a son of the prophets, cries, "The wrath of God is revealed . . . against all ungodliness and wickedness." And Jesus? On countless occasions he is so angry he's livid. If he were not livid, he wouldn't be loving. Elie Wiesel, Jewish survivor of the Holocaust, repeats in virtually all his books that the contradiction of love is not hatred but indifference. If our Lord were indifferent he could not love. The fact that he is angry proves he cares. And to say that he cares is to say that he loves.

From time to time people tell me they're upset as they read through the written gospels, for on many occasions Jesus doesn't seem genteel. Correct. He isn't genteel. On many occasions Jesus uses language that would take varnish off a door. Like the time he spoke of Herod as "that fox." When we modern folk read "fox" we think of sly, cunning, devious. But "fox" as a metaphor for sly or cunning comes out of the eighteenth-century English sport of fox-hunting. Jesus was never an eighteenth-century English sportsman. In first century Palestine "fox" was the worst thing you could call anyone. "Fox" bespoke anger and loathing rolled into one. Today we would say "that snake, that skunk, that weasel" (not to mention what we might say if we used less polite expressions). Our Lord said it and he meant it. His vocabulary on other occasions, we might as well admit, was no different. But — and a huge "but" it is — the people who fire our Lord's anger *he will die for*. For them he will die that incomprehensible death of God-forsakenness precisely in order to spare them it. And he will do all of this inasmuch as he and the Father are one; which is to say, love is his essence, his pure nature as well.

The prophet Habakkuk cries to God, "In wrath, remember mercy." To remember, in Hebrew, doesn't mean to *recollect the idea of*. In Hebrew to remember means to *act on the basis of*. To remember mercy is to act on the basis of mercy. Habakkuk's cry to God is answered in the cross: in the midst of his wrath God has remembered his mercy. For wrath is love burning hot as it reacts to our sin, while mercy is love bringing blessing as it forgives our sin.

God is joyful

Joy floods God himself when his love for us achieves its purpose and we lose ourselves in love for God. Nasty people attack Jesus on the grounds that he welcomes irreligious people and even eats with them. He in turn tells his accusers why he welcomes such people and eats with them. The parable of the lost sheep concludes with the declaration that there is joy in heaven over one sinner (even just one!) who repents. The parable of the lost coin concludes with the declaration that there's joy before the angels of God over one sinner who repents. Of course joy floods God at this; for in the repentance of one sinner his fathomless love has achieved its purpose and has quickened uncalculating love for him.

I should never deny that repentance entails — must entail — what St. Paul calls "godly grief" (2 Corinthians 7:10). I should never pretend that repentance is possible without sober, oft-times tearful, recognition that a wrong road has been pursued and pursued for a long time. I should never deny that the heart that is newly acquainted with its iniquity and infidelity can be other than horrified at itself. Nonetheless, repentance doesn't remain *fixed* in godly grief. Ultimately repentance is self-abandonment. It is abandoning ourselves to a love so vast that we're left unable to do anything else. Repentance is finding ourselves overtaken and saturated by a love so far-reaching that we forget our hurts, wounded pride, petty grudges, self-serving ambition and childish vendettas. We forget it all inasmuch as we're taken up into the very love that has taken us over.

I'm sure you've noticed a tantrum-prone two-year-old clutching in his fist what he believes supremely important, never to give it up. The more he's asked to give it up the more his childish defiance hardens and the more tightly he grasps it. If you try to pry it out of his hand he will explode and then sulk and then make everyone around him miserable. When will he give it up? When he's offered something more attractive. Before God we adults have the spiritual maturity of the two-year-old. We hold fast our hurts, grudges, self-promoting schemes. When the preacher rails against us and tells us we should let them go we only hold them more tightly, even become irritable. We shall abandon them not when we are chided but when we are overwhelmed by a love so vast as to quicken a love in us which gladly leaves behind all such childish encumbrances.

The prophet Isaiah knew of God's joy at the homecoming of his people. "As the bridegroom rejoices over the bride, so shall your God rejoice over you."

When next you wonder who or what God is, repeat one simple line: "Love with every passion blending." Repeat it until it goes so deep in you that the love of which it speaks — God's love — quickens in you an identical response to him: namely, *your* "love with every passion blending."

Chapter 21

BEARING THE BEAMS OF LOVE

As a Christian it's impossible to "love safely";
we enter it undefended or not at all.

*Can we really remain
detached when working
and living with people?
When our gut gets hooked
we must follow through.
As we grow in our
capacity to endure love's
beauty and pain, we're
able to carry love,
even magnify it.*

I played hockey for 12 seasons. Though I never weighed more than 155 pounds I regularly played against 210-pound gorillas who were as mean as junk-yard dogs. I survived the 12 seasons inasmuch as I always knew how to protect myself on the ice. I took to heart the advice Ted "Scarface" Lindsay gave to Stan Mikita when Mikita moved from junior hockey to the NHL. A smaller fellow, Mikita had voiced his fear that he wasn't tough enough to play in the NHL. Lindsay said, "As long as the stick is in your hand you are as tough as anyone on the ice. Never drop your stick!" I soon learned that a deft two-hander applied even to a Gorilla's unprotected ankles (the referee does not see ankle-high infractions) conveyed my message unambiguously and left me unmolested.

Because I could always protect myself on the ice I was all the more surprised to learn, years later, that I could not protect myself politically. I was as defenseless as a first-time skater standing on wobbly legs at centre ice: unable even to get out of the way, never mind run down anyone else.

Subsequently I learned that not only could I not protect myself politically, I couldn't protect myself psychologically. I seemed to get bushwhacked emotionally in a way most people seemed to avoid, or at least disguise. I seemed unable either to avoid it or disguise it.

I concluded that I had to learn to protect myself. Detachment was to be my first piece of armour. "Be laid back," I told myself a dozen times over. "Be detached; stay cool; keep your gut unhooked." It all went exceedingly well, and I thought I was really progressing at remaking myself psychologically; it all went well, that is, for three hours. Then the phone rang. A 43-year-old woman had called me from the Credit Valley Hospital out-patient department. She needed a ride from the hospital to work and wanted to talk to me. She was riddled with tumours, as skinny as a broom handle; her skin-colour was a ghastly yellow-brown, and she was struggling to keep a marriage upright that seemed close to capsizing.

End of detachment. End of being laid back. Gut hooked all over again. Then I recalled the words of Gerald May, M.D., an American now living in Washington, who has written much in the field of spiritual direction. (A spiritual director is someone who helps individuals discern and assist the movement of God's grace within them.) Professionally May is a psychiatrist who served, at one time, with the United States Air Force in Viet Nam. In one of his many books he has written, "Some wisdom inside us knows it is impossible to love safely; we either enter it undefended or not at all."

We can't love safely; either we love defenselessly or we don't love. Instantly I admitted to myself what I had known in my heart all along, despite my short-lived efforts at detachment and coolness: a disciple of Jesus Christ whose preoccupation is survival is no disciple at all. Dr. May is correct. We can't love safely.

Next I pondered the two lines from the poet, William Blake, which May quoted in his book, *The Awakened Heart.*

And we are put on earth a little space
That we might learn to bear the beams of love.

Gerald May says only three things about this quotation. We are to bear love in the three dictionary senses of "bear": We are to grow in our capacity to endure love's beauty and love's pain; we are to carry love and spread it around — "as children carry and spread measles and laughter," he adds; and we are to bring love to birth. When I read this I was so very startled that I didn't move. Instead my mind spun out what it is to *bear love* in this three-fold sense.

Enduring love's pain

First, we must grow in our capacity to endure love's beauty and love's pain. Love's beauty we understand. But love's *pain*? Does love pain? Yes. And in my older age I have come to see that beauty brings with it its own pain.

When the Shepherds were last in England we traveled into the Yorkshire moors. Everyone has some picture of the moors, thanks to the writings of the Yorkshire veterinarian, James Herriott. He has not exaggerated. We Shepherds walked together upon the moors as the sun was setting. I shall not attempt to describe it. Suffice it to say it was so beautiful as to leave us dumbfounded. The beauty was so exquisite as to border on the surreal. In the next instant the beauty seemed so intense as to make us ache. The beauty surrounding us contrasted so very sharply with the unbeauty we find on so many fronts in life that this wordless beauty brought with it a peculiar kind of pain.

In the midst of the unlove we find on so many fronts in life we are startled when we find ourselves loved with a love whose intensity is beautiful, to be sure, and whose beauty makes us ache. When we are loved not because we are useful to someone else or because we're needed or convenient; when we're loved for our own sake, loved for love's sake — this is when we learn what it is to endure the exquisite beauty and ache of love.

It's easy to confuse love with other linkages. My children love me; they also need my funds for university education. My wife loves me; she is also legally bound to me. My mother loves me; she is also old and sick and has made me executor of her will and granted me power of attorney. What's more, all of these people to whom I am related by blood or marriage would be considered perverse, nasty, deficient themselves if they didn't love me. At the same time, none of this means they don't love me for my sake, love me for love's sake.

Still, there are circumstances where the love with which we are loved can *only* be love for our sake, love for love's sake, because we're not linked in any way to those who love us. I marvel at the love with which I am loved when this or that person will never profit from my estate, never be the beneficiary of my life-insurance, never have any legal tie to me; when in fact there is no material, social or employment advantage — no advantage of any kind in loving me. Yet they continue to pour upon me a love whose beauty is so beautiful as to make me ache. Not only is there no advantage accruing to them; there is every disadvantage! I have embarrassed them in public on occasion. I have committed social gaffes in their presence which left them wishing (for a few minutes, anyway) that I was at someone else's party. I have plunged them into emotional anguish just because they were so closely identified with me in my emotional anguish. And I have perplexed them as they stood speechless before my incomprehensible spasms of irrationality.

The longer I live the more amazed I am at all of this; I must grow in my capacity to cherish and endure it; to not flee it, not find it so strange as to be foreign, not resist it inasmuch as I cannot control it, not allow its glory to be diminished by its singularity.

We must bear love in the sense of growing in our capacity to endure its beauty and its pain.

Spreading love

Second, we are to bear love in the sense of carrying love and spreading it. Surely we are to do so chiefly unselfconsciously. There are situations where we have to clench our teeth and resolve that hatred will not burn up our love. There are days when we have to fight the temptation to hate as surely as our Lord fought assorted temptations in the wilderness. But we can't be fighting all the time. We can't have our teeth clenched and our resolve clothesline-taut all the time — or else we should be as grim as death!

Ever since Louis Pasteur published his discoveries we have known about the transmission of communicable diseases. Such diseases move throughout the human population by means of germs; invisible to the naked eye, but no less real for that. In a fallen world disease is naturally contagious; hatred is too. No one has to be taught to hate; left alone, humankind does it naturally in this era of the Fall. Then love can be spread only by an infusion of God's Spirit. Only the Spirit (everywhere in scripture the Spirit is the *effectual* presence of God) can cause the love we pour out on others to do something besides run off them like rain slicking off an umbrella. Only the Spirit of God can cause love to stick to others, to penetrate, to swell, and to declare that love has brought forth its increase in someone who is (like us all), in some measure, love-deprived.

The body's immune system is a good thing. It keeps us from falling sick with scores of different diseases in the same day. Yet there is one place where our immune systems are counter-productive: when we need a heart-transplant. Here it has to be overridden, or we shall reject the one thing we need most.

We human beings have an immune system, as it were, of a different sort as well. It keeps us from being "suckered" by every last fad, ideology, scheme or deviousness. And yet there is one place where our beneficial immune system (which renders us rightly suspicious) must be overridden by the Spirit of God if we're not to reject love. Only God himself can do this. And this is precisely what he has promised to do. We shall leave him to do it, even as he leaves us to what we must do: bear love in the sense of carrying it, spreading it.

Bringing it forth

Third, we are to bear love in the sense of bringing it forth. Once again this is something we cannot do ourselves. Just as we cannot make our love for others adhere to them, so we cannot of ourselves quicken love in them, bring forth in them that love which is now love *from* them. Of ourselves we cannot render someone else a loving person. Once again only God can; and he has promised to do this as he takes up and honours our unselfconscious commitment to people who find in our commitment to them what they have found nowhere else.

When Gerald May was with the United States Air Force in Viet Nam he worked in the psychiatric ward of a military hospital, then returned home where he worked in a prison and in a state psychiatric hospital next. Working in these three venues occupied 20 years of his life. He says these years were bleak. Every day he drove to work wondering what on earth he thought he was doing. For instance, every day he spoke with a woman, a patient in a state hospital, who never said a word. She appeared so vacant as not even to notice him when he was speaking to her. Still he didn't ignore her (it's difficult not to ignore someone who is utterly unresponsive) but did his medical duty by her, changing medications and writing up charts. This situation continued for six months. One day, in the course of the same hospital routine, he was fishing in his jacket pockets for a "light" when this unspeaking woman walked out of the room into the corridor and silently beckoned a nurse to her. "Dr. May needs matches for his pipe," the psychotic woman *said*. Only God can bring love to birth; and God does precisely this as he takes up and honours the commitments we make to others.

Unquestionably Jesus Christ bore love in the threefold sense of "bear." He most certainly received love from others; he endured that love which is so exquisitely beautiful as to ache. When the adoring woman poured on his feet the costly perfume he remarked, "She has done a beautiful thing to me . . . she has anointed my body beforehand for burying" (Mark 14:6,8).

Just as certainly Jesus carried love, spread it, as the gospel writer attests: "Having loved his own who were in the world, Jesus loved them to the end" (John 13:1).

And just as certainly Jesus brought love to birth. Matthew was a

SEASONS OF GRACE: from Wilderness to Wonder —

tax-collector who had sold out to Rome and now stood to gain financially by collaborating; Simon was a zealot, a terrorist who had vowed the assassination of every last collaborator he could safely stab. What kept these two men in the same apostolic band except the love which Jesus had brought to birth in both? What else kept Jews and Greeks in the same congregation when Greeks had always regarded Jews as anti-intellectual and inflexible while Jews had always regarded Greeks as bereft of God and shamelessly immoral? What else keeps together a congregation gathered in one fellowship?

You and I are to "bear the beams of love," in the words of the poet. We *can* bear love in the three-fold sense of enduring its beauty and pain, spreading it, and committing ourselves to those in whom God will bring it to birth just because Jesus Christ has done it already and done it in us.

SUMMER

Temptations in the Wilderness

We find almost irresistible the more subtle,
"righteous" sins that can take us down as
swiftly as the big ones.

Chapter 22

THE POWER OF OUR WORDS

*We underestimate the power of our words to create realities
— for good and for ill.*

*The Israelites understood
the link between words
and actions. When God
spoke, something
happened. Our words too
can build up or destroy.
They must "fit the
occasion" and, motivated
by love, impart God's
grace to hearers.*

"Sticks and stones may break my bones but names will never hurt me!" They won't? Someone else's tongue can't hurt us? Ask Captain Dreyfus. Albert Dreyfus was an officer in the French Army at the turn of the century. He was Jewish. The under-the-surface antisemitism that is never much beneath the surface broke through. The name Dreyfus was called was "traitor." There was no foundation for the label. Dreyfus was accused nonetheless. Then he was tried, shunted aside and shunned for years, only to be tried again. Eventually he was exonerated. But his exoneration meant little. By now his military career was in ruins, his life a shambles, his family devastated. In addition the "Dreyfus affair," as it came to be known, unleashed a wave of lethal antisemitism throughout France. Not only did the one word "traitor" destroy him, it traumatized thousands of others as well. It was as if one stone only had been thrown into the water, yet the ripples were as unending as they were countless.

How did you feel the last time you were lied to or lied about? You were hurt grievously. How did you feel the last time you were not lied to or lied about but were publicly humiliated nonetheless?

We must always remember that the command not to bear false witness is found in that section of the Ten Commandments that also forbids theft, adultery and murder. False witness is clearly every bit as damaging. Theft is robbing someone of her goods; adultery is robbing her of her spouse, the most important creaturely relationship; murder is robbing her of her life. False witness does any one of these, or any combination of them, or even all three at once.

Words create events

A word, once uttered, is not merely a grammatical unit. The spoken word is an event. The Hebrew language honours this truth, for the word *dabar* means both "word" and "event." Our Hebrew foreparents knew that the chief characteristic of God is that he speaks. They knew too that when God speaks something happens. It's not the case that God speaks, then silence swallows up his word as though it had never been uttered, with the result that nothing significant has occurred. God speaks, and the universe with its inexhaustible complexity is fashioned out of nothing. God speaks, and the prophets themselves are "voice-activated." Elijah, Ezekiel, Jeremiah and Isaiah were prophets whose entire existence was "voice-activated" by the Holy One of Israel. Amos acquaints us with the irrefutable ground of his vocation: "The Lord God has spoken; who can but prophesy?"

Jesus, the Word of God incarnate, utters that Word which he himself is, and Lazarus is quickened from the dead. Jesus sends out his disciples to many different towns. They are to preach in his name. If their word (his word) is not heeded in this or that town, says the master, "it shall be more tolerable on the day of judgement for the land of Sodom and Gomorrah than for that town." In short, to disdain and dismiss those words that attest Jesus Christ and his kingdom is to guarantee one's non-survival in the coming judgement. *Dabar*: the word is an event.

It's difficult for us twentieth century-types to grasp this because we think speech and act are entirely distinct. Speaking is speaking and acting is acting. They are as unlike as sunbeams and creamed cheese. We have to work at thinking our way back into a Hebrew understanding where speaking and doing are *one*. Imagine yourself standing alongside the Grand Canyon; standing alongside it, but not too close, for suddenly a word is uttered. In that instant the jagged outcroppings of rock are crumbled and the canyon floor is filled in as hills and valleys are leveled. Difficult to grasp? No! After all, we use ultrasound to pulverize kidney stones, don't we? Our familiarity with this procedure helps us understand the psalmist when he writes, "God utters his voice; the earth melts." Word and event are one: *dabar*.

The purpose of speech

If we think about this for a moment it's obvious. One purpose of speech is to disseminate information. If I am told that Paris is the capital city of France or Lake Superior is the coldest of the Great Lakes or the sun is 93 million miles from the earth, then more than speech has occurred: ignorance has been dispelled. That's the event in this case: ignorance has been dispelled, and the foundation for greater learning has been put in place. More profoundly, another purpose of speech isn't merely to disseminate information but also to be that vehicle that conveys us ourselves in our self-giving to another person. The words, "I love you" don't merely disseminate information; they are the vehicle that conveys the speaker herself in her self-giving to another person. Word and act are one.

A moment's reflection on the power of dysfunctional speech reminds us terrifyingly of what speech does. Sarcasm, for example, is contemptuous, biting speech whose aim is the opposite of what the words mean. The baseball hitter strikes out with the bases loaded in the ninth inning. As he stumbles back to the dugout, head down, a fan shouts, "Well done, all-star!" The words mean that the batter is a superior player who has just performed outstandingly. What the fan intends to say, however, is the exact opposite: the hitter is an incompetent who belongs in the lowest level of the minor leagues. And it is all said with deliberate intent to wound.

The child brings home his report card with a glaring "D" in arithmetic. His mother can't help noticing it and comments, "I see that you are another Einstein; my child is a genius!" The meaning the parent intends is the exact opposite of the meaning the words have, and the intent is to hurt the child. The child *is* hurt, stabbed in fact. A psychiatrist-friend tells me sarcasm destroys children, simply destroys them. (It doesn't do much to help adults, either.) The child understands the meaning of the words, yet also notes anger and rejection in the speaker's voice and on her face; the child is wholly confused by the contradiction and knows at the same time that he has been stabbed in the heart.

Humorous speech is often a form of dysfunctional utterance. The purpose of humour, ostensibly, is to amuse. But often humour is used to ridicule or mock, to taunt and taunt until the taunted person explodes and lashes back. Whereupon the taunter, insisting the purpose of his humour is never to upset, smirks self-righteously, "I always knew that fellow had a bad temper!"

Sometimes humour is used to cloak a dagger-thrust. Person *A*, with malice in his heart, wants to say something nasty to person *B*, without exposing himself to retaliation. If *A* simply spoke nastily, *B* might turn the tables on him and with superior verbal skill demolish *A* in a devastating counterthrust. *A* decides to cloak his dagger-thrust in humour. If *B* replies sharply, *A* takes refuge in his humour saying, "I was only being funny; can't you take a joke?" On the other hand, if *B* pretends to "take the joke" and says nothing, he knows he has been stabbed and can't do anything about it! When humour is used not to amuse but rather to leave a victim defenseless, speech has been used dysfunctionally with terrifying power.

The bluntest, baldest form of dysfunctional speech, of course, is the outright lie. A lie, by definition, corresponds to nothing substantive at all. A lie, therefore, is like a vacuum which, by definition, is nothing. Yet, like a vacuum, a lie has immense power. The worst feature of a lie isn't that misrepresentation has occurred (serious though this is); it's that the person telling it can no longer be trusted; forgiven, yes, but never trusted. What is lied about may be of little importance; the fact that someone can no longer be trusted couldn't be more important.

The so-called "white" lie, "white" in that the teller intends no malice but is simply taking an easy way out of a sticky situation, has the same end-result: utter breakdown of trust. Many people have told me white lies thinking they were sparing my feelings. But why spare my feelings at the price of forfeiting trust? The people we find lying to us we can forgive and engage politely thereafter. But it would be unreasonable to trust them.

It is little wonder that the apostle James speaks so severely of the tongue. While the biggest ship or horse can be directed by the smallest rudder or bit — any man or woman being able to control the small bit or rudder — no man or woman can direct his or her life by controlling the smallest tongue. The tongue escapes human control, with the result that the whole person careens dangerously and disastrously like a rudderless ship or a bitless horse. In only 12 verses James tells us that the tongue is a fire, is a stain which stains the entire body, is a match which ignites huge conflagrations, is itself set on fire from hell, is a restless evil, is as untameable as the wildest animal, is as full of deadly poison as a cobra. James gathers up all his teaching about the tongue by naming it "an unrighteous world." The tongue is a world. "World," for James, always means the culture and institutions of the universe organized without God and as such the antithesis of the kingdom of God. Think of it: the sum total of the universe's culture and institutions, sunk in ungodliness, organized to oppose God's kingdom — all of this concentrated in three inches of flexible tissue. Little wonder that grace is needed; grace and grit. God's grace is needed if we are to have the capacity and the desire to do something better; our grit, our determination, our resolve are needed if in fact we are going to do something better.

Speaking the truth

The men and women upon whom Jesus Christ first stamped himself knew what we must do. First, we must speak the truth. This is simple. I didn't say easy; to speak the truth in a world of mendacity is never easy. Jesus insists that the evil one is a liar and a murderer. This is no surprise; to be a liar is to be a murderer. We have already seen how the liar slays; the liar slays trust, therefore slays relationships, therefore slays people. Liars are killers. Since God imparts, sustains, redeems and fulfills life, his people must always choose life rather than death. Therefore we speak the truth.

It is important that we speak the truth, important as well that we *speak*. In the church we hear endlessly of the sin of speaking when we shouldn't, yet we hear nothing of the sin of remaining silent when we should speak. Everything James says about the tongue's hyperactivity applies as well to the tongue's inertia. After all, when the truth is known but not spoken, then falsehood triumphs. I have come home from church-court meetings sick and heartbroken at the silence of clergy who knew in their hearts what the truth was but who remained silent at critical times. Next day they have phoned me and said, "Victor, we have read the stuff you write; we agree with what you said last night; we are with you all the way." But at the critical moment they were so fearful that they phoned me next morning lest they be seen talking to me. Silence, let us remember, is a form of speech. When a false statement is met with silence, the silence is a left-handed way of expressing agreement with the statement, however false.

James insists that the tongue is an unrighteous world; silence is too. The unrighteous world is the only world the world knows. But Christians do not aspire to ape the world; we aspire to that kingdom that cannot be shaken and that unfailingly contradicts the world. Therefore we speak the truth, giving equal weight to both "truth" and "speak."

Speaking with love

In the second place we are to speak the truth in love. "Truth" describes the content of what we say; "love" describes our motive for saying it. Our motive is never to bludgeon or mislead. Since love "builds up," according to the apostle Paul, our motive in truth-telling must be edification alone. And if the truth wounds temporarily, it must only be a surgical wound, a last-resort necessity to promote life.

Lastly our truth-telling must "fit the occasion," says the apostle, "so that it may impart grace to those who hear." There is always the fitting occasion for saying what we have to say. Only as the truth is spoken and heard in the appropriate context does it impart grace; only here will it reflect the word of the God who comes to save rather than destroy.

The God who comes to bind saved people to himself, inviting them to bind themselves to him, will always be their God. He promises them, even as he invites them to promise to him, lifelong love and loyalty, gratitude and obedience. All of this recalls the covenant. The covenant, biblically, is God's declaration that he wants a holy people so badly he will give himself, holding nothing back, at whatever cost to him, to free and woo and win a people for himself. That people he has freed and wooed and won through blood-shed grace; so grateful are they that they abandon themselves to him and henceforth live in eager, cheerful obedience to him, reflecting in all of this his own lifegiving goodness. This is the covenant.

In scripture the covenant is celebrated with salt. The offerings God's people bring to worship are sprinkled with salt. The incense burned in the temple is seasoned with salt. Not surprisingly the Hebrew Bible speaks of God's covenant with his people as "a covenant of salt" (Numbers 18:19; 2 Chronicles 13:5). When an Israelite baby is newly born it is rubbed with salt, a sign that this child, born into the covenant people, must be nurtured so as to grow up reflecting the lifegiving goodness of God himself.

With this much salt before us we can grasp immediately what Paul means when he tells the Christians in Colosse that their speech is to be "gracious, seasoned with salt." Salty speech is speech that befits the people of the salt-covenant. The speech of God's covenant people is to embody the lifegiving goodness, death-defeating goodness, of the God who comes only to save. "Let your speech always be gracious, seasoned with salt . . . ."

Eight hundred years before Paul many people complained to the prophet Elisha that the spring-water in the city of Jericho was rendering the people of Jericho infertile, unfruitful. Elisha poured salt into the spring and declared, "Thus says the Lord, I have made this water wholesome; henceforth neither death nor miscarriage shall come forth from it."

According to Elisha's descendant, Paul, we who are God's covenant people are to speak in such a way that our speech brings forth not death, not even something which betokens life yet finally emerges dead; our speech is to embody the lifegiving goodness of him who is the world's only saviour and therefore its only hope.

Chapter 23

THE PATHOLOGY OF ENVY

Envy causes us to spin out of control. What is the cure
for this fatal condition?

*Envy poisons, embitters,
blinds us. Just as the
aerobatic pilot must
continuously re-orient
himself to the ground,
so we must ceaselessly
re-orient ourselves to
that ground which is
God, all the while
rejecting the distractions
of the world's trifles.*

*E*very winter people injure themselves — some seriously and a few fatally — through slipping on ice. They are most likely to slip when they don't see the ice and are unable to safeguard themselves in any way. The ice has been covered over by the thinnest layer of snow or by a discarded newspaper. Before they know it their feet are gone from underneath them and they lie immobile, wondering if the pain in the elbow, shoulder or wrist betokens a broken bone. If they've struck the back of their head they may be beyond wondering anything, at least for a while. Having one's feet slip unexpectedly is no small matter.

What happens with our feet around ice happens to our self, our total person, around life. We slip and fall dangerously. Painfully. Catastrophically. Having slipped we have to ascertain how much damage has been done to us and how long recovery will take.

The psalmist tells us he came within an eyelash of having his feet slip catastrophically when envy invaded his heart. "My steps had well nigh slipped. For I was envious of the arrogant, when I saw the prosperity of the wicked."

Envy is a sin which threatens us all and of which we are all ashamed. Nobody boasts of being envious. People do boast of their sin, to be sure, but not the sin of envy. Some people (chiefly males) boast of their lust. They think advertising their lasciviousness exalts them as red-blooded "studs." Some boast of their hair-trigger temper. They think advertising their rage exalts them as no-nonsense types who don't take any "guff" from anyone. But no one boasts of envy. Envy is devious. Envy is always disguised. It's always denied outwardly however much it consumes us inwardly.

Envy is subtle. Have you ever noticed the extent to which it can be disguised as social justice? For years I've noticed that often what's put forward as concern for the poor is frequently envy of the rich. Attempts at lifting up many is secretly the attempt at pulling down a few.

Yet not even pulling down a few satisfies our envy, simply because envy can never be satisfied; the more it is fed the more its satisfaction recedes.

Why are we envious?

Why are people envious? We envy inasmuch as we assume anything someone else has we too must have. Likely we never even wanted the thing until we noticed another person has it. Suddenly the fact that he possesses it and we don't is intolerable.

Further, we refuse to admit there are people who genuinely have greater talent, intelligence or skill than we have. We think that to acknowledge someone else as more talented or intelligent is to declare ourselves failures (when of course it is to declare no such thing).

While none of us needs any encouragement to envy we are "encouraged" nonetheless on all sides. Think of the advertising beamed into us every day. So much of it aims at fostering in us a desire for what someone else has. Did she not have it, or did we not know that she has it, we shouldn't want it for ourselves. (I'm not speaking here of genuine human need but of artificially induced want.) We are pressured from all directions with the message that unless we have something too we shall remain sunk in inferiority. What we want we soon expect. When expectation is not fulfilled, want is riddled with anger and resentment; blended together these appear as envy.

Envy poisons friendship

For this reason the most tragic aspect of envy is the poison it injects into friendships. Envy swells in us concerning those people whom we consider equals. No one of our social class envies Queen Elizabeth, even though she is the richest woman in the world. Instead we envy our dear, dear friend, whose job pays him $25,000 per year more than we earn. Suddenly he appears less dear. In fact he now displays character-defects either he didn't display before or we didn't see. But it's more a case that we've recently come to imagine them and even project them. All the while we remain unaware of what's going on in our own head and heart. It is plain that his good fortune has left us feeling belittled. He never intended to do so; in fact his $25,000 per year hasn't belittled us. Nonetheless we are certain now he is belittling us, as certain as we are that the sun rises in the east. Feeling ourselves belittled we stupidly think — yet think nonetheless wickedly — we can restore ourselves to our proper size, our proper largeness, only by diminishing him. Envy is always bent on leveling. End of friendship.

Envy poisons us

As surely as our envy poisons our friendship envy also poisons us personally. It renders us forever uncontented, therefore forever unable to rejoice. Languishing in self-rejection, we feel dejected. Worse, since envy renders us sour, the more other people try to love us out of our envy the more we curdle their every effort.

"My feet had almost stumbled," cries the psalmist. "I nearly fractured both legs, plus spine and skull; I nearly rendered myself immobile and insane when I became envious of the prosperous, for I looked upon the prosperous as arrogant and wicked." It may be that the prosperous are arrogant or wicked — at least some of them, but perhaps no more than anyone else. At this point the psalmist's envy has rendered him ridiculous. Prosperous people, the psalmist whines, "have no pangs." They don't suffer? They aren't as finite, frail and fragile as the non-prosperous? Ridiculous. We often like to think the prosperous "have it made." Because they're protected against financial loss we assume they're impervious to human loss. Their lives are devoid of difficulty, every bit as trouble-free as we foolishly imagine them to be.

Always at ease?

"Always at ease," the psalmist says of the prosperous, "they increase in riches." They may increase in riches, but are they "always at ease"? Think of the well-known Kennedy family. Corrupt? Joseph Kennedy made millions handling liquor during the era of prohibition. Wicked? The extramarital affairs of sons John and Robert, not to mention their simultaneous affair with Marilyn Monroe, scarcely describe them as virtuous. The family had no pangs? Two sons assassinated, Ted Kennedy's wife an alcoholic, a grandson who is a drug-abuser, another family-member charged with rape, the early demise of "Jackie O."

And even if, in another case, there is no moral failure attached to someone who is prosperous, it still isn't true the prosperous are pang-free. John Robarts, lawyer, former premier of Ontario, suffered a stroke that left him partially paralyzed, and in his despair he shot himself.

Envy blinds us to a person's suffering. We assume that whatever it is about him that is enviable has rendered him invulnerable, impervious to suffering, one hundred percent affliction-proof. But of course the prosperity of the prosperous cannot protect them against the human condition.

Envy also renders us self-pitying, self-righteous snivellers. "All in vain have I kept my heart clean," the psalmist whines in his envy. "I have kept my heart clean and received nothing for it!" The truth is, he hasn't kept his heart clean. His hands may be clean (he hasn't done anything wrong), but his heart? How can he pretend it's clean when he envies those whose prosperity (he says) has filled them with despicable character-defects? Insofar as he envies them he is plainly willing to become a despicable character himself as long as he gets rich at the same time.

It is little wonder that no one boasts of envy. Who would brag that he has turned himself into a poisonous, embittered, blind, self-righteous whiner? Not even the psalmist is going to boast.

A moment of truth

What happens to him next? In a rare moment of rationality and self-perception he realizes how grotesquely he has disfigured himself. In the same rare moment he realizes how shabby he appears to his fellow-believers, his congregation. "I should be untrue to the generation of thy children," he cries to God. The New English Bible puts it most succinctly: "Had I let myself talk on in this fashion I should have betrayed the family of God." Plainly, the light is dawning.

But he needs more than the dawn; he needs broad daylight in order to get himself straightened around. Broad daylight floods him *when he goes to church.* "I went into the sanctuary of God," he tells us. He worshipped. To worship is to adore someone infinitely greater than we, and therefore to have our sights raised above ourselves. To worship is to be oriented *away* from ourselves. Just because we're envy-prone and self-preoccupied we need to be re-oriented again and again, *at least* every seven days (the bare minimum).

Few spectacles delight me more than air-shows. Aerobatics entrance me. The formation-flying of the Snow Birds or the Blue Angels is good, but I prefer the solo performances of the smaller, propeller-powered aircraft. These small planes perform far tighter maneuvers, and much closer to the ground. Recently I saw an aerobatics display on television that included film-footage of the pilot. The pilot had been photographed by a camera positioned at the front of the cockpit. As the plane rolled and twisted and flipped upside down I noticed the pilot was looking for the ground every two seconds. He was constantly re-orienting himself. Because his maneuvers were so extreme and so sudden he could easily lose his bearings; and because he was so close to the ground he had no margin of error. He re-oriented himself — "Where's the ground?" — at least every two seconds; otherwise he would crash.

In the course of everything that comes upon us, including the insane envy all of us know but will not admit, we too roll and twist and flip upside down. The only way we can keep from crashing is to re-orient ourselves constantly by looking for that "groundedness" that is God. To re-acquaint ourselves with "groundedness" is to avoid the crash. Worship is essential for this; if not every two seconds then at least once every week.

As the psalmist goes to "church," as he worships, he gets his bearings once more. That rare moment of rationality and self-perception that drew him to church and secured his bearings asserts and extends itself and gradually dispels the envy with its spinoffs that had so recently laid hold of him. He returns to his right mind. He can scarcely believe how absurd he had become and how seriously he had warped himself. "I was stupid and ignorant," he cries to God. "I was like a beast toward thee."

"Not only was I asinine," he tells us frankly, "I was even outrageously insensitive to God; and for the longest time I couldn't even see it!" As his envy evaporates his self-perception returns. He knows he has been on the edge of catastrophe himself; he has come within an eyelash of betraying his fellow-believers, and he has affronted God.

The thoroughness of the psalmist's re-orientation is given by his exclamation, "Whom have I in heaven but thee? And there is nothing upon earth that I desire besides thee." Martin Luther's translation is priceless: "As long as I have thee, I wish for nothing else in heaven or on earth." As the psalmist's life sinks more deeply into God's life; as God's life sinks more deeply into the psalmist's, the vastness of God floods the psalmist again and dilutes his envy until it vanishes without trace. "As long as I have thee, I wish for nothing else in heaven or on earth."

How do we come to want less?

Someone might wish to say that the cure for envy is to want less. Of course to want less is to do away with envy. But to say this is as unhelpful as to say the cure for sickness is to be without disease. The critical question is, "How do we come to be without disease?" "How do we come to want less?" By repeating 100 times per day, "I resolve to want less!"? This would only remind us of all we don't have and leave us wanting more! We cease wanting more by *forgetting* the "more" we don't have. We forget it as we become preoccupied with him who himself is "more"; so much more, in fact, that to be possessed of him is to see the world's trifles as just that: trifles which feed our acquisitiveness and vanity but never satisfy them.

"God is the strength of my heart, and my portion for ever," says the psalmist at the end of his 73rd tract. One thousand years later another son of Israel, born in the city of Tarsus and soon to die in the city of Rome, wrote, "For me to live is Christ; and to die can only mean more of him, for ever."

Psalm 73 is a study in the pathology of envy, as well as a declaration of deliverance from the fatal condition. While we have allowed the psalmist to tell us much, however, we are going to let someone else have the last word. The writer of the Book of Proverbs says, "Contentment is a feast without end" (Prov. 15:15, Jewish Publication Society).

Chapter 24

THE RIGOURS OF SPIRITUAL DISCIPLINE

Without the most intensive training we shall find ourselves disqualified.

Training in godliness is required for temptations that assault us. We can't afford to be soft, self-indulgent or ill-prepared. A soft, lazy streak remains in us, the hangover of our sinnership. Discipline will help develop a spiritual sixth sense to intuit what's before us.

It was always the last thing we did in the gym, when we were so tired we could barely remain upright. We stood with our feet together, looked at a spot on the wall, and then rotated our head as widely as we could, over and over, all the while concentrating on that one spot on the wall. At first we all became dizzy and lost our balance. Gradually we were able to keep standing and looking at that spot in front of us, regardless of our dizziness.

We were boxers in training. The coach said the point of the exercise was to train us to keep looking at our opponent unthinkingly after we had been staggered by a blow and the lights were going out and we were dizzy. "This little exercise will keep you alive one day," he told us, "and you will thank me that I insisted you do it."

He was right. The day came for all of us — and came more than once — when our training kept us looking at our opponent when we'd been hit and the ring was reeling.

Boxers aren't the only people who get rocked. Everyone does. Including Christians. One day temptation hurls itself upon us so violently that we can only call it assault. Another day misfortune hits us when we're not expecting it at all. Or disappointment plunges us sickeningly as fast as a skyscraper elevator plummeting out of control. The worst blow of all, the solar plexus punch that can leave us in terrible pain, conscious yet helpless, is betrayal — there's no blow like betrayal.

It's plain that Christians need training. St. Paul calls it "training in godliness." The apostle had already seen how important training is for the athlete. He referred several times in his epistles to the rigorous preparation which the boxer, wrestler and runner undergo. If they can't afford to be soft, self-indulgent or ill-prepared, he said, can the Christian be any less?

Training in godliness is necessary, something we have to keep working at until that day when, says Peter, we are crowned with that "crown of glory which never fades."

All of this may sound a bit too intense for you, even grim. But it isn't! Why is it so necessary?

Our fallen nature demands it

Christians are indeed those who are "born of the Spirit," in the vocabulary of the New Testament. As Jesus Christ embraced us in his grace we embraced him in faith. We were reconciled to God, given a new standing before God, and a new nature as well, or, as scripture speaks of it, a new heart. None of this is pietistic verbiage. We *are* possessed of a new name and a new nature.

Nevertheless, as Martin Luther liked to say, the old man, the old woman, doesn't die readily, doesn't die without a struggle; the corpse twitches. We mustn't forget that Jesus instructs *disciples* to ask for forgiveness every day just because sin still clings even to disciples. To say that Christians are identified before God as new creatures is not to say that the old creature has disappeared; while the old creature is not our identity, it is a twitching corpse which can still trip us up.

When I was younger I thought my depravity was relatively

slight, always in sight, and therefore easy to keep at bay. Much older now, I am sobered, even horrified, upon being confronted with the sewer-element that remains in me. Sewer too strong? What word would you prefer when our Lord himself says, "What comes out of a man is . . . evil thoughts, fornication, theft, murder, adultery, coveting, wickedness, deceit, licentiousness, envy, slander, pride, foolishness." This is what effervesces up out of us. The Christian who says, "It would never be found in me" is ignorant and a fool as well. What's more, the Christian who insists she is beyond any effervescence of her depravity is three minutes away from proving to the world how wrong she is.

As sin-riddled as we undoubtedly are, can you imagine how we'd look if we were devoid of spiritual discipline? Spiritual discipline will be needed for as long as we are Spirit-born children of God whose identity in Christ is contradicted by the hangover of our sinnership. Then spiritual discipline will always be needed. St. Paul insists that without the most intense training the athlete will find himself *disqualified* (I Corinthians 9:27).

The conflict without

Spiritual discipline is needed not only because of what remains "in here"; it is further necessary because of the spiritual conflict that rages "out there." Let's make no mistake. Our Lord insisted he came to do battle with the evil one. All through Christ's public ministry he is opposed. He contends with his foe for every inch of ground his foe has illegitimately occupied. No occupier retreats willingly; he or she must be routed. In other words, Christ's ministry is unrelenting conflict.

Christians are those whom the master has enlisted. We are *soldiers* of Christ, as the New Testament is unashamed to say. But what use is a frontline soldier who has never been trained? Not only what use is he; how long is he going to last?

During the last war there were two aspects to the training of a submarine commander. One aspect was becoming schooled in the technicalities of submarine warfare: when to launch a torpedo, how close to the target one should be, what to do in assorted emergencies. The second aspect was much more subtle, more intuitive, more a matter of sixth sense: whether to surface or remain submerged; whether to fight or flee; whether to wait for moonlight or wait for cloudcover.

The technical aspect could be learned quickly out of a book. The second, life-or-death aspect was much harder to come by and took far longer to acquire. At the beginning of the war young submarine captains had time to learn the latter aspect. Towards the end of the war there was no time. Not having acquired the subtle intuitions which a submarine commander needs to survive, these fellows didn't survive; neither did the crews entrusted to them. They perished in record numbers. A great many of them drowned on their first voyage.

So it is with the Christian life in the midst of spiritual conflict. It's easy to acquire a Christian vocabulary, easy to gain a rudimentary grasp of Christian doctrine. But it takes far more time, far more diligence to gain a spiritual sixth sense; to intuit whether what has been thrust in front of us is an opportunity to be seized or a danger to be avoided, whether what is proposed in the document before the official board is kingdom-building or kingdom-destroying.

Since keeping company with Jesus Christ means that his venue of ministry is also ours, and since his venue is ceaseless spiritual conflict, we need spiritual discipline. Without it we shall be of no use to him; without it we shall not even survive ourselves.

A cutthroat world

Spiritual discipline is needed for another reason. The world in which we live is a tough place. The world resists truth, righteousness, love. The world is populated by billions of people, every one of whom is fallen; the world seethes with concentrated self-interests; clamouring, competing self-interests, even cutthroat self-interests.

I was asked to attend a meeting in order to support a non-profit housing organization which was to build a facility to accommodate *eight* head-injured adults recovering from head-injuries sustained through automobile accidents, industrial accidents, and occasionally athletic mishaps. They would be housed for approximately six months, after which they'd be able to function without special provision.

Many people went to the meeting. No doubt in other contexts they would appear decent, considerate, even moderately compassionate. But on this night they were determined that the head-injured of Mississauga could freeze to death before they should be housed in their neighbourhood. If you had ever doubted that the world is a tough place you would not have been doubting at the conclusion of that meeting. Some people implied that those who have suffered head-injuries (concussions) are slobbering ogres or rapacious molesters around whom no one is safe. Others said that whether dangerous or not, head-injured people are unsightly and would detract from the handsomeness of the neighbourhood.

Whereupon I asked these people if they thought they could spot a concussion walking down the street. I was not thanked for my question. The woman beside me complained bitterly that the increased traffic would be a huge nuisance. "Increased traffic?" I remarked, "there are only eight people to be accommodated, and none of them can drive!" She turned on me in her fury: "So what if they can't drive; would you want them living on your street?"

A city councillor, who had called the meeting, appeared to support the proposal. A few days after the meeting a representative from the housing organization told the councillor that since the housing organization had already spent $75,000 on preparatory work, it had to know, before it committed any more money, whether the councillor was going to support the proposal officially. "Not only am I not going to support it," the councillor said in an apparent about-face, "I am going to bury it!"

Christian life, Christian service — every aspect of our discipleship unfolds in a world that is tough, even treacherous. Spiritual discipline is needed if we are going to do anything besides give up.

To forestall discouragement

I've already anticipated a fourth reason for spiritual discipline: to forestall discouragement and capitulation. It must not happen! It won't happen only as long as we have anticipated it, prepared for it, and stand equipped by the training or discipline which keeps us looking ahead even when we have been rocked.

Components of spiritual discipline

Then in what does spiritual discipline consist? The first item is prayer. John Calvin was right when he said, "Prayer is the chief exercise of faith." God commands us to pray. Faith recognizes the command of God and is eager to obey him. Not only does faith recognize the command of God; it understands the command of God, it knows that God wills only our blessing. Then God's people must pray consistently, pray habitually, pray believingly.

Even if we were slow to understand this it would be difficult to overlook the example of our Lord himself. He prayed, and prayed, then prayed some more. He prayed in marathon sessions before major developments in his life (for example, the calling of the twelve). He prayed with others in public in the synagogue where he worshipped every Sabbath. He prayed alone on countless occasions. The written gospels depict him going away to a "lonely place a great while before day," in order to be alone and to pray. What our Lord knew to be essential we cannot pretend to be optional. Since prayer is the chief exercise of faith, believing people are equipped chiefly through prayer.

To be sure, spiritual discipline includes ethical rigour, intellectual strictness and psychological resilience. But of themselves these will never equip us spiritually. Then if spiritual discipline is what we need above everything else we must pray. Apart from it our Lord himself would plainly have had no ministry, no life. We cannot do without the very thing which he knew to be his lifeline.

Utter self-honesty

The second requirement in spiritual discipline is self-honesty — *utter* self-honesty. The older I become the more sobered I am at humankind's capacity for self-deception. People whose minds are logically rigorous will find that once they are tempted their logical rigour becomes rigorous rationalization. The logic is still there, but now it serves their self-justification. The very thing they were counting on to safeguard them against the seduction of temptation now reinforces the seduction. Thinking that their logical rigour would safeguard them against being dragged into sin, their logical rigour now prevents them from being argued out of sin. Our capacity for self-deception is bottomless.

One could ask, "If self-honesty is essential, and yet our capacity for self-deception is bottomless, how are we going to arrive at the self-honesty we need?" With the help of two instrumentalities. One is scripture. Scripture is the normative witness to Christian faith and life, to what we must believe and do. Scripture is also a mirror. When we look into it we begin to see where, why and how we have deceived ourselves with respect to our faith and our discipleship. Corrie ten Boom, the Dutch woman who survived Ravensbruck, the camp from which so few women emerged, managed to smuggle a small pocket Bible with her when she was incarcerated. She read to her fellow-inmates night-by-night, and expounded the text as well. After a while a woman who was not a believer (or at least who hadn't been when she was locked up) said to Corrie, "That book of yours; it is the only book that tells us the truth about ourselves."

Spirit-sensitive friends

Another instrumentality by which we penetrate our self-deception is the company of Spirit-sensitive friends. For years I thought I had privileged access to my own heart and mind. I thought I knew more about myself than anyone else could know about me. When it was suggested that this was not the case I became very defensive and insisted that it was. It was only after much embarrassment and anguish that I came to admit that there are settings in which other people know me far better than I know myself. In such settings these people have something to tell me about myself that I should be a fool to ignore; in ignoring them I should not only embarrass but endanger myself. For this reason I shall always need, as you will too, one or two or three soul-mates who are spiritually sensitive, spiritually attuned; friends who are willing to tell us truth about ourselves with respect to which we are self-deceived; friends from whom we can hear this without falling into denial, excuse-making, and silly defensiveness.

The venue of service

The last item in spiritual discipline is service, especially service in a venue which appears to contradict the truth of God and the reality of his kingdom. Two decades ago the students of the Oxford University Humanist Club hung a huge banner over the doorway of a theological college: "For God so loved the world that — last year 37,000 thalidomide babies were born." A low blow? Not really. Spiritual discipline has to be tested; it is tested in the midst of developments which appear to contradict the God for whose service our discipline is preparing us.

Such testing will always be essential. A military unit can train till it turns blue. Yet no amount of training can substitute for combat experience. The soldier really becomes a soldier when he is under fire. Spiritual discipline bears fruit and proves itself fruitful when we are under fire. We are then of even greater usefulness to God in the service of that world which he will not abandon however much it may contradict him.

Our enthusiasm for spiritual discipline is the measure of our seriousness as disciples of our Lord Jesus Christ.

Chapter 25

WHY DO PEOPLE LEAVE?

Hardship induces many people to exit the faith, but so does "softship."

Jesus asks us, as he did he twelve, "Do you want to leave too?" People leave because they find Jesus' teachings too hard. Adversity dashes cold water on faith. The flame flickers and goes out. How can we learn to persist in faith even in the wilderness?

Crowds are fickle and easily swayed. A rabble-rousing speech can turn a docile crowd into a dangerous mob in only minutes. And even where the crowd is not dangerous, it can still be led to behave in a way individuals in the crowd never would. We need only recall the sober, sensible, middle-aged women who thronged Nathan Phillips Square several years ago. Pierre Trudeau turned them into a crowd of 15-year-old hero worshippers whose fantasy-lives were never more lively.

Occasionally I used to watch debate programs on TV, one of the precursors to today's talk shows. I noticed that the crowd frequently reversed its opinion after listening to a clever speaker (not profound) for only 20 minutes.

Jesus attracted crowds. But he never trusted them. Crowds were large; followers remained few. On one occasion a crowd was swept off its feet as he spoke, impressed by him at the same time as it misunderstood him. Its misunderstanding was glaring: it tried to make him king. The crowd wanted to make Jesus their revolutionary leader.

Jesus refused. He knew that while politics is important, it's not ultimately important. What is important, said Jesus together with the prophets before him, is a new heart — a new love and loyalty, a new manner of thinking and faculty of discernment as well as a new road to be walked, new resources to be claimed, new confidence in God's future for God's people.

Political revolution is certainly understandable; it may even be necessary (some would say). But while it changes the players in the game, *it never changes the game itself!* It interchanges ruler and ruled, but it cannot transform the human heart. Jesus knew his mission was to unloose the powers of the age to come, as the Book of Hebrews puts it, and to bring men and women to "taste" the powers of the age to come. Jesus refused to be heralded as the leader of the people's revolution; he knew that at bottom it was no more to be trusted than the tyrant's tyranny. He wouldn't allow himself to be sidetracked.

Appropriation of truth

Yet while the crowd was in front of him he *would* speak to them. "Unless you eat my flesh and drink my blood, you have no life in you," he cried. He wasn't referring primarily to the Lord's Supper, but to what the Lord's Supper points to. Eating and drinking are Hebrew metaphors for the innermost appropriation of truth. "Unless you receive me, cherish me, get me into your bloodstream, you are spiritually lifeless." Now the crowd was furious. Of course it was! Who wants to be told she is spiritually inert? "This is a hard saying," the crowd griped and grumbled, "who can listen to it?" The Hebrew word "listen" or "hear" always has the force of "obey," "heed." "This is a hard saying; who can heed it, take it to heart?" Whereupon the crowd turned away from Jesus. If the crowd likes what you say, you're a hero; if it doesn't, you're a bum. One minute the crowd hailed Jesus as the leader of the people's revolution. Next minute it deserted him as too harsh to be heeded.

Not only did the crowd desert him, John tells us, so did many of our Lord's followers. They went looking for someone easier to follow. Jesus turned to the twelve and asked, "Do you want to leave too? Now's your chance! Do you want to leave with the others?" Speaking for the twelve Peter replied, "Leave? Where could we go? To whom could we go? You have the words of eternal life!"

Why people leave

The question Jesus put to the twelve he puts to us. "Do you want to leave too?" As a matter of fact people do leave. Why?

Some disagree vehemently with our Lord's assessment of humankind. We are irked, even exasperated and angered, when Jesus persists in telling us, "Unless you eat my flesh and drink my blood — unless you *receive* me, your saviour — you have no life in you; you're spiritually inert."

"But we are good people and we do good things!" This is not in doubt. At the same time our very goodness becomes the shield behind which we hide from God; our very virtue is the achievement to which we point to demonstrate that we don't need a saviour; our very goodness justifies our resistance to the God who wants to invade us and invigorate us.

What's more, our goodness, good as it is, is still only a good veneer. In the wake of the Fall human goodness, civilization, humanism is only one millimetre thick. Once this millimetre is ruptured savagery appears.

All of us have seen pictures of emaciated men in the Serbian prisoner-of-war camps, men whose every rib can be counted and whose skulls are so fleshless their eyeballs appear ready to fall out. Rosie, the proprietor of Pastry Villa in Mississauga (I do 80 per cent of my pastoral counselling in Pastry Villa), is a Croatian Muslim. She was telling me recently of her people's children who have been found with their throats cut.

Elie Wiesel, a survivor of the holocaust, appeared on TV in connection with the Yugoslavian atrocities. Sadly Wiesel commented, "In 45 years humankind has learned nothing." Of course it has learned nothing. Humankind learns nothing precisely because, disdaining our

Lord's "unless," humankind assumes it need learn nothing.

Fifty years ago a group of physicians, leading medical researchers, performed the most dreadful medical experiments without benefit of anesthesia on concentration camp inmates. Not to be outdone, the Allies refused to bomb the railroad tracks that conveyed doomed people to the death camps. Why? Because we were glad enough to let someone else annihilate the people the world despises. Scratch civilization skin-deep and we are looking at savagery.

As we read St. John's account of the people who heard Jesus and then left him we should ask ourselves: do we agree or disagree with our Lord when he says, "unless . . ."? This question is bedrock. It concerns our most elemental relation, our relation to God. It also concerns our elemental assessment of humankind. In the wake of the Fall, to resist Jesus Christ on this point means not merely that humankind won't be godly; it means it ultimately won't even be humane.

You may say people who make a religious profession are no different, no better. But Jesus is not urging us to parrot a religious profession thoughtlessly. He is insisting we have to have him, his truth and especially his way as deep inside us as DNA. And of course we have to receive our Lord not once but afresh, as often as we breathe. A suspicious woman who doubted the Christian standing of my friend, Bob Giuliano (a former minister at Erindale United Church), asked him if he had ever been born again. "Many times," said Bob thoughtfully, "many times." We must keep on appropriating our Lord, learning of him, and keep on being corrected by our sisters and brothers in faith.

The bottom line in all this is whether or not we agree with our Lord's diagnosis of humankind. Some people then found it too extreme, too severe. "A hard saying." They left. Some people leave today for the same reason. They simply disagree with our Lord's diagnosis of the human heart.

The cold water of adversity

Other people leave for a different reason. Adversity dashes cold water on their faith, and the flame of faith seems to flicker and go out. I should never make light of someone else's hardship or what it has done to her. If someone tells me life has tumbled in on her in such a way that the rubble has blotted out her sense of God's presence, I cannot contradict her. I understand why she says she has left.

At the same time I'm aware some people appear to be struck by adversity every bit as heavy, yet do not leave. Moderate pain seems to induce some people to give up on our Lord, while severe pain finds other people trusting him more than ever. I have no sure-fire explanation of this. I only know some people feel life's beatings have rendered our Lord's word unbelievable. The adversity that renders Jesus Christ less than credible need not be their own. It can be someone else's adversity they observe. Let's not forget that one-quarter of all children under age five in Somalia have died as a result of famine or civil war.

Preoccupation

A third reason people leave is that they're simply preoccupied. In his parable of the sower and the seed Jesus speaks of the seed of the Word of God which falls on thorny ground. "They receive the Word," says Jesus, "but the cares of the world, the delight in riches, and the desire for other things choke the Word."

You and I live in an ocean of affluence. For generations now real per capita wealth, in North America, has doubled every generation. My wife and I are twice as wealthy as our parents, four times as wealthy as our grandparents. We are awash in affluence. Not only are we distracted by the trinkets and toys we can purchase, the wealth itself does more than merely distract; it renders us superficial, self-satisfied and cocky. Superficiality will overtake any one of us unless we deliberately resist the desire for "other things" and the "delight in riches." Where it isn't resisted, there is but a short, downward step to saying "There is no point to faith, it means nothing to me, it has come to be one more item of clutter in my busy life."

North American affluence is plainly an instance of softship.

Softship is far more likely to seduce us away from our Lord than is the hardship of the world's afflicted.

As the crowds and some followers left Jesus he put the question to the twelve: "Are you going to leave too?" Peter's reply was swift and sure: "To whom shall we go? You have the words of eternal life!" Immediately Peter added, "We have believed, and have come to know, that you are the holy One of God." The Greek verb tenses have to be read carefully. Peter's reply has this force: "We have come to believe — and now stand firm; we have come to know — *and our conviction is unshakable* — that you are the holy one of God, you have the words of eternal life, and it would be the height of foolishness for us to look anywhere else."

Have you ever noticed we are so turned off by the religious know-it-all that we uncritically assume it's better to be a know-nothing-at-all? But it isn't better. While the know-it-all is certainly obnoxious, the know-nothing is unfailingly useless; he simply can't help anyone. Peter and the others were not flaunting themselves as know-it-alls when he spoke; yet they were just as far from being know-nothing-at-alls. "We know, and our conviction is unshakable, that you are the one whom our hearts fit and our heads meet and our hands must ever hold."

It is our experience of our Lord, not merely doctrinal familiarity or biblical sophistication, as important as these are, but an experience tested in many fires and shining ever more brightly that gives us something to say and do. Without such experience of our Lord we can only listen to other people's confusion, fear, superficiality and hopelessness, only then to reflect it all back to them. If we're going to be that light "that gives light to all in the house," according to Jesus, then we must enlighten — and we can do this only as we're constrained ourselves to say with Peter, "We have come to believe, we know . . ."

The gospel makes sense

Recently I've noticed that the older I become, the more sense the gospel makes. Far fewer "problems" surround believing the gospel now than when I was younger. (Then the gospel struck me as true yet somewhat problematic. Now it's the world's self-understanding that strikes me as problematic because false!) The odd thing about this is that my experience is the opposite of my society's. Secularization means the gospel makes less and less sense to our friends and neighbours. It's only as the gospel makes more and more sense to the church that the church will have any real or effective place in our society. And the gospel is going to make more sense to the church only as it first makes *some* sense; that is, as the church owns the treasure entrusted to it and finds itself urged to say from within its heart, "We have come to know, with unshakable conviction, that you are God's very presence and power; you have the words of eternal life; we have validated this in our own experience time without end; and we should not think of looking anywhere else."

Three kinds of people

Consider the three kinds of people in the crowd who leave off following our Lord. First were those irked by our Lord's diagnosis. Here we can only wait for the day when their reflection on life leads them to see that his diagnosis is correct. And because it is correct, it's not oppressively negative but in fact startlingly positive, utterly hopeful, since it is the first step of their recovery.

Then were those whom "softship" has preoccupied. We can only wait until a shaft of light shines so brightly that it pierces the insulation of their softship and strikes home.

Finally there are those whom adversity has trampled. There is much we can do here. Gentleness and sensitivity are needed at all times. Concrete help may be in order much of the time. In their adversity they will know we have not abandoned them. Our not leaving them in their adversity will be a sign, *the* sign, that the One whose disciples we are has not abandoned them either. Knowing this, they will leave off leaving off, and will follow him, along with us, once again.

SUMMER

The Wonder of God's Invigoration

Jesus' teachings invigorate us.
We spend a lifetime learning them, and in the process
realize it's the Master himself who matters.

Chapter 26

THE MARK OF A CHRISTIAN

Grace-induced boldness is a distinguishing mark of the Christian.

Boldness gives us confidence to approach the throne of grace and authorities of all kinds, as well as the principalities and powers Christ has triumphed over.

What one word says the most about the Christian life? Most people would say love, or faith, or perhaps discipleship. In the Book of Acts, however, the single word most frequently used to speak of the Christian life is *boldness*.

Christians speak boldly, act boldly. The Greek word *parrhesia* resembles shot silk, a textile dyed a particular colour — blue, for instance. As light falls on the blue silk from different angles, the colour takes on slightly different hues: blue-shiny, blue-flat, blue-grey, blue-black. It's still blue, but because of the shot silk it's always a variegated blue, a colour with constantly changing nuances depending on the angle at which light falls on it as well as on the angle of vision.

So it is with the word "bold": but not in the sense of cheeky, pushy, nervy or smart-alecky, which only put people off. There is nothing to commend a boldness that is little more than rudeness.

In Acts the apostles are said over and over to speak and act boldly, frankly, openly. A dozen different English words are used in any translation to convey the one Greek word that describes the public demeanour of Christians. There is a forwardness about them that isn't cheeky, a directness that isn't discourteous, a forthrightness that isn't insensitive, an outspokenness that isn't saucy, a bluntness that isn't brutal, a plainness that isn't brazen, a confidence that isn't cocky. *This* characterizes Christians, says the book's author, Luke, even as it first characterized him who is the Christian's Lord.

The Book of Hebrews exhorts us, "Let us with confidence [boldness] draw near to the throne of grace that we may receive mercy and find grace to help in time of need."

No one can doubt our need of mercy and help in times of hardship. We are sinners whose sinnership is so deeply ingrained that by comparison deep-seated medical problems appear almost superficial. We are chronically needy people whose fragility is constantly exposed. Every day we are clobbered by someone's heavy artillery, infected with someone's poison, caught off guard with a surprise attack. The fact that we are in need of mercy and help, however, doesn't guarantee that they are available. Yet it is the promise of the gospel that what we cannot generate ourselves God supplies out of his sheer kindness.

Occupied by grace

As we look to God, says the Book of Hebrews, we see that the sovereign's throne is *occupied by grace*. Most people expect a throne to be occupied by power — sheer power. If they're lucky, such power might be slightly benign. After all, in the history of the world a benevolent sovereign has been so rare as to render his subjects exceedingly fortunate. But the throne above all thrones is occupied by *grace*. This takes my breath away. My life, your life, is ruled, ultimately, by grace.

Because grace *rules*, it is not a useless warm fuzzy as ineffective as a pipe dream. Grace penetrates, permeates, achieves what it alone can. At the same time because it is *grace* that rules, that "Other" to whom we look and in whose presence our lives unfold is neither an arbitrary tyrant nor a heartless judge. From my first to last breath, my life — with all its convolutions and subterranean murkiness — is comprehended by grace. Therefore I can look to God knowing he wants only to bless me.

Further, since grace is sovereign, I can look to God knowing nothing can impede the blessing he wills for my life. Then I must always *with confidence* draw near to the throne of grace.

The author of Hebrews insists there is only one ground of our assurance that grace rules and therefore one ground of our confident drawing near to the throne of grace. It is that Jesus Christ, the Son of God, has withstood all the assaults that render us prone to collapse and all the temptations that render us prone to corruption. Resurrected and ascended, he has been crowned sovereign. It is entirely reasonable to draw near with utmost confidence, for now we know we shall surely find mercy and help.

Our confidence is not cockiness. Still, we have been emboldened to approach expectantly the only ruler the world has, and know we shall be met with grace and nothing but grace.

Before the authorities

The angle of vision changes slightly and the same word takes on a slightly different hue. Peter and John were hauled up before religious authorities. The officers, who prided themselves as religious experts and procedural masters, assumed they would be able to humiliate, dismiss or punish the two disciples of Jesus whose faithfulness to him had landed them in trouble. They were surprised to find something about Peter and John they couldn't quite put into words, something they couldn't do anything about, but which they also couldn't deny. Luke wrote, "When they saw the boldness of Peter and John, and perceived they were uneducated, common men, they wondered; and then they recognized that these two had been with Jesus."

Uneducated, common — yet bold! In first-century Palestine "uneducated" meant "without formal rabbinical training," or "without a degree in theology." "Common" meant "having no professional status." Yet these two men were possessed of something ecclesiastical authorities couldn't handle; and whatever it was that possessed them, it arose from their having been with Jesus.

The boldness of Peter and John was not cockiness. It was

conviction plus courage plus transparency. Living in the company of Jesus supplies this.

I am the last person to belittle learning of any kind, especially theological learning. At the same time, a pastor's having passed an examination in theology will never benefit his congregation unless he has been with Jesus and continues to be. Congregations that are discerning know this: they're not fooled. For eight years I sat on a committee that assessed candidates for the ministry. It included clergy, businesswomen, teachers, others holding postgraduate university degrees. Many of them struck me as naive about who should or should not be ordained to the ministry and entrusted with a congregation. But there was one kind of person who was never fooled: the middle-aged homemaker with the slenderest formal education. She was never taken in by big words, paper credentials, letters of recommendation or impressive-sounding arguments. She intuited the appropriate boldness of the candidates who had been with Jesus. She was able to recognize its presence or absence inasmuch as she pulsed with it herself.

I profit enormously from scholars who genuinely are scholars; I enjoy the rich mental furnishings and intellectual stimulation. After all, scholars excite fellow-scholars. Yet as often as I like to think I'm a scholar I remember I'm always a needy human being; a fellow-sinner and fellow-sufferer with all humankind, whether scholarly or illiterate.

When I need help more than I need stimulation I look to those who are "uneducated and common." They have neither formal training nor professional status, yet they sustain, nourish and encourage me. Such people, for me, are the sober alcoholic, the person addicted to anything at all who has come to know great deliverance, the mother of the disabled child whom nothing and no one except our Lord has kept unbitter and unresentful for years, the parishioner who could never preach a sermon yet understands her pastor's struggle and encourages him through his bouts of emotional spasticity.

Nothing can take the place of having been with Jesus. Professional standing and formal training are categorically distinct. The church authorities who attempted to stampede Peter and John learned this. There is a courage, a transparency, a non-belligerent boldness that comes only through intimacy with our Lord.

Simple starkness

The angle of vision changes slightly and the root word "bold" now has the force of *simple starkness*. The disciples assumed Lazarus was sleeping. They talked about going to wake him up. Jesus said plainly, "Lazarus is not asleep; he is dead."

Divorce is painful to contemplate, painful to endure. It's a word we prefer not to use. Biblically speaking, divorce is a manifestation of death. Let's not pretend anything else. Pitiable as marriage-breakdown is, when a marriage is dead the only realistic thing to do is to say in a loud voice, "This is *dead*." Jesus was every bit as plain with respect to Lazarus. He does not lend us a religious softening of realism; instead he insists we confront reality. Simple starkness always befits a frank acknowledgment of reality.

A family dinner conversation one night swung around to Christ's driving the fleecers out of the temple. Mary, 16 at the time, asked, "Did Jesus seek forgiveness for what he did?"

"No," I replied. "There's no suggestion Jesus had any awareness of sin or guilt in himself."

"But he acted violently," Mary came back.

"Not only was he violent," I added, "his violence was premeditated. He didn't walk into the temple, observe the exploitation of defenseless people, then lose his temper. Jesus *braided the whip* from a handful of cords. He spent ten minutes doing this, thinking about what he was going to do once he had finished."

Next question at the Shepherd supper-table: "Is premeditated violence ever justified or required on the part of the Christian?" It is painful to contemplate such a question. No doubt it is far more painful to *do* violence. Nevertheless, Jesus frankly directs us to recover realism.

So I told my children of Dietrich Bonhoeffer's complicity in the plot against Hitler, knowing that if Hitler were removed thousands of Allied and German lives would be spared. We talked about the role of police departments, of United Nations' forces, even the role of the school principal in forcibly expelling the student who assaults other students or teachers. There's no point in pretending we live in a Pollyanna world where such situations do not develop. Christ directs his people to own the realism of these situations.

"Lazarus isn't sleeping; he is *dead*." Our Lord speaks boldly and bluntly not to brutalize his hearers, but to keep them from hiding their heads in the sand unrealistically. He does as much for his followers today.

Principalities and powers

Change the angle of vision once again and another nuance of "boldness" appears. Paul says of Jesus Christ, "He disarmed the principalities and powers and made a public example of them, triumphing over them." Note: his actions were public, open, manifest. In beating the principalities and powers he did so boldly. Principalities and powers are any of the influences and forces that give us personal identity and public identifiability. This force can be genetic. "He's retarded," we say, as though the boy's humanity and significance were exhausted by his inability to do long division. It can be corporate. The company you work for fires you. Company executives leave you feeling you're a failure; the manner of your dismissal publicly advertised you as a failure. Failure is now your public identifiability. The force can be racial. "She's black, you know, really *black*." Or ethnic: "They are Chinese." Or social: "He is wealthy." In every case there is a private identity and a public identification.

Then there are people who work for a company or belong to an institution that truly gives them a mind-set and character-set in conformity with the institution itself. They have been *made* this — and usually are entirely unaware of it.

The truth is, I am not *any* of the things I am thought to be. I'm not what belonging to an institution has made me to be. I'm not any of the things my friends, employers or upbringing have made me. I'm not even the sum total of all the influences and forces that have pressed themselves upon me — simply because Jesus Christ has *vanquished* all of these, and vanquished them boldly. By faith I am a *child of God*, a person whom only God knows so well as to know who I really am. This of course can be said of any Christian. Nonetheless, I am not "any Christian"; I am that child of God whose identity is entrusted to God and will be made plain to me and others on the day of our Lord's appearing.

It is enough for now that I know myself to be that one whose identity is vouchsafed to God and preserved inviolate by him. It is enough that I know myself to be that child of God for whom there can never be a substitute, upon whom inestimable love and patience are poured, and with whose Father I am destined to live eternally. I can know this on the ground that Jesus Christ has made a public example of those influences and forces that he has conquered. Through his resurrection he has boldly displayed them as bested. Nothing will ever be able to deflect me from who I am before God.

Christians are called to glorify in the description *bold* . . . .

It means *confident* but not cocky in our approaching that throne whose grace rules our life as well as the entire world.
It means *bold* yet not brazen in our transparency to the Lord whom we know and cherish.
It means *stark* as we own the realism of life.
It means *public*, open, manifest as we recall our Lord's triumph over everything that gives us a false identity and false identifiability.

This one word has sustained me for years.

Chapter 27

FROM ELIJAH TO JOHN
AND DAVID TO JESUS

What can we learn from the intensity of Jesus, his cousin
John the Baptist, and their forefathers, Elijah and David?

*These men were "lit":
torched by the God who is
a "consuming fire."
Impassioned, often
unpolished in their
preaching, praying, rage
and dejection, they teach
us much about our
cowardly compromises.
We're to get right, do
right, live right by God.*

*M*y appetite does not improve when I see a crow pecking at a dead animal on the side of the highway. And if a crow were to drop a bit of ragged roadkill in my lap I should be repulsed. Elijah the prophet was told to hunker down by the brook Cherith, which flows into the Jordan, and crows would feed him there. Feed him what? Everyone knows what crows eat.

Elijah looms out at us from the Bible as a man who is utterly God-saturated. Over and over we're told, "The word of the Lord came to Elijah" — and off Elijah goes to do and say what has been laid on him.

Clearly, the prophet was God-soaked, for the text explains him entirely in terms of the God who has inundated him. He was humble — it takes more than a little humility to allow oneself to be fed carrion. He was courageous — it takes enormous courage to speak truth to political or ecclesiastical powers, particularly when that power (King Ahab and his cruel wife Jezebel) is murderous. He was unpolished — subtlety and soft speech were foreign to him.

Most notably he was impassioned. Wherever we find Elijah his passion is aflame: his preaching, praying, scorn, rage, dejection — all are a conflagration. Moderation? Balance? The "golden mean"? He wouldn't understand. We wonder why Elijah is always and everywhere afire; he wonders why we appear not to be lit.

The greatest of the Hebrew prophets according to Jewish opinion both ancient and modern, Elijah was God's spokesperson in the face of the Baalism that surrounded Israel and threatened to infiltrate it. Baalism (both ancient and modern) is actually nature-worship, conveniently lacking any grasp of evil or sin. Nature-worship will always attract the hordes who want religion without ethics. Not surprisingly Baalism tolerated, even encouraged, lasciviousness of all sorts.

King Ahab, an Israelite who knew exactly what God meant when he insisted he is a "jealous" God (God abides no rivals; worship of him cannot be mixed with worship of anything else); Ahab nevertheless thought he could have his cake and eat it too. Why not mix together Baal, the pagan deity, and Yahweh, the true and living God? Why not have the self-indulgence Baal permits his people and the security Yahweh promises his people? Why not the fornication Baal laughs about and the forgiveness Yahweh weeps to bestow? Don't the television preachers tell us repeatedly that God wants us to "have it all"? That we can have all the "goodies" of the world together with the gospel of God?

Elijah rightly says, "No, a thousand times no!" And so we find Elijah, the prophet of God, standing amidst the 450 prophets of Baal. "The Holy One of Israel," Elijah says to them, "will shortly expose your Baal for the inconsequential puff of smoke that he is. And as for you, Ahab, so far from being a real king you're a double-crosser; you've betrayed the very people whose spiritual protector you were commissioned to be." Whereupon Ahab stabs his finger at Elijah, "You troubler of Israel; why do you have to be such a disturber?"

Jewish people always knew that Elijah would come back at the end-time when the kingdom of God was breaking in on the world, as the "Age to Come" was superimposed on what Israel called the "Present Evil Age." When he came back he would do four things: restore people inwardly through repentance, gather together the scattered people of God, proclaim salvation, and introduce the Messiah.

The Baptist: a man with a mission

Centuries later John the Baptist appeared. He didn't eat carrion brought to him by crows; he ate honey made for him by wild bees, with grasshoppers added for protein. John too spoke truth to lethal political power. This time it was to King Herod, a Jew in name only who had sold his soul to pagan Romans and now betrayed the very people whose spiritual protector he was commissioned to be. And just as Elijah had ringingly denounced Ahab's theft of Naboth's vineyard, so John denounced Herod's theft of his brother's wife.

John had an elemental message he declared tirelessly: "Repent. Right now. Don't say, 'Tomorrow.' You don't have tomorrow. The axe is laid to the root of the tree. Get right with God *now*. How will anyone know if your repentance is genuine? By the subsequent shape of your life. Will baptism in the Jordan (or anywhere else) save you? No it won't. Unless your life is reordered before God, getting yourself baptized in desperation is no different from a snake slithering away in panic from a grass fire."

Then John began gathering together the scattered people of God. He urged repentance even upon soldiers, despised gentiles as they were, with the result that even they were added to the "household of faith." In the same breath John proclaimed the salvation brought by his cousin, Jesus, whose shoelaces John felt himself unworthy to untie. Did he introduce the Messiah? Repeatedly John urged the people, "Don't look at me; look at him. He is the one to baptize you with the fiery Spirit of God!"

Months later the detractors of Jesus taunted him, "You can't be the Messiah. Everyone knows Elijah must come back before the Messiah can appear. And Elijah hasn't returned for 800 years!"

"Wrong again," said Jesus to his detractors. "Elijah *did* come back. Recently. And you made fun of him. You called him 'the dunker, the dipper.' You dismissed him. Did not John urge repentance, gather the scattered people of God, declare the salvation of God and introduce the Messiah?"

Jesus Christ, the Messiah of Israel and the saviour of the world, is nothing less than the mirror-image of God himself. We can receive Jesus Christ only as we first hear and honour the word of the forerunner, Elijah and John compressed into one.

David and Jesus: born to be kings

They both came from simple country-folk — David and Jesus. Both gained notoriety when they were still adolescents: David the shepherd boy who accidentally "showed up" older men when they wouldn't respond to Goliath's challenge, Jesus as a 12-year-old who stymied learned clergy in the temple.

They both possessed enormous backbone, neither one a pushover, neither one cowering before brute power. When David saw the terror that had paralyzed his countrymen in the face of Philistine threat he scornfully said of the leader, "Who is this uncircumcised Philistine that he should defy the armies of the living God?" When Jesus knew Herod wanted to terminate him he scornfully said to whoever would listen, "Go and tell that fox . . ." (As noted earlier, fox, in first-century Middle-Eastern street-talk, was shorthand for the most loathsome "creep" imaginable.)

They both showed mercy to their enemies: David, when he knew Saul wanted to kill him yet let him go, Jesus, when he prayed at the last, "Father, forgive them, for they don't know what they are doing."

They both were men of passion. When David exulted without restraint "before the Lord," his wife, Michal, despised him for it. When the passion of Jesus fired his public ministry and rendered him heedless of danger his mother thought him deranged and wanted to take him home and sedate him.

Both were fighters, both declined the weapons everyone else assumed they ought to use. David was offered Saul's armour, but put it aside, trusting a simple slingshot and the use God would make of it as God honoured the one who had first placed his trust in his Father. Jesus, summoned before Pilate, told him he had at his command legions of angels whose unearthly power could have vapourized Pilate on the spot, together with everything Pilate represented. Instead Jesus trusted a simple cross and the use his Father would make of it as his Father honoured the one who had first placed his trust in his Father.

Both David and Jesus were born to be king. David was born in Bethlehem (literally, "house of bread"), a village outside Jerusalem. One thousand years later Jesus was born in Bethlehem too. Most Israelite kings simply lined their pockets and slew their opponents. David was different. He knew that an Israelite king had three responsibilities: to protect the people, uphold justice, and serve as a priest.

A military genius, David protected his people and upheld justice. Justice today means little more than seeing that criminals are convicted and sentenced. Not so with that justice which God decrees. In the Hebrew language, there is no word for justice; the Hebrew word is judgement. The king as God's agent was to uphold *God's judgements*. God's judgement is not primarily a matter of convicting criminals and sentencing them, but rather, God himself setting right what is wrong, freeing those who are enslaved, relieving the oppressed, assisting the helpless, clearing the name of those slandered and vindicating the despised.

David did this. Those who had been set upon were set upon no longer. Anyone who "fleeced" the defenseless or exploited the powerless learned quickly that King David had zero tolerance for such abuse. When David himself was fleeing Saul's murderous hatred 400 men and their families gathered around David, "everyone who was in straits . . . in debt and . . . desperate." To be desperate is literally to be without hope; to be in straits is to have no escape. All such people found in this king one who would never disdain, ignore or abandon them.

And priest? The role of the priest was to intercede with God on behalf of the people. Frequently David went into the tabernacle "and sat before the Lord." The people were on his heart; he pleaded with God for them all.

A blind beggar minutes away from receiving his sight called out to Jesus, "Son of David, have mercy on me." "Son of David" meant *Messiah*. The Messiah was to be a great king, greater even than David. A blind man could see what sighted people could not see and knew Jesus to be the long-awaited king greater even than David.

The protection Christ the King gave, and continues to give, his people is more glorious than any protection David furnished, for Christ our King has promised that nothing will ever snatch you and me out of his hand; nothing will ever separate us from that love of God made concrete in the King himself.

That Son of David who is Christ the King upholds justice as he implements God's judgements. Jesus himself said that all judgement had been delivered over to him. Since the primary purpose of judgement is to restore the right, to say he is judge is to say that he is saviour. If the primary purpose of the judge is to set right anything that is wrong, *anywhere*, from the sin of a child to the disfigurement of the cosmos, then the judge has to be the saviour as well.

And priest? In his atoning sacrifice Christ the King uniquely pleads with the Father on behalf of the people. For this reason the Book of Hebrews speaks of Christ the King as "our great high priest."

Where they differ

But when it comes to the matter of sin, the paths of David and Jesus diverge. The New Testament tells us that Jesus was "tempted at all points as we are, yet without sin." David was also "tempted at all points," but he sinned grievously. He lusted after Bathsheba, Uriah's wife. His lust warped his thinking. Adultery-on-the-way rendered murder perfectly reasonable. David didn't merely stumble; he sprawled ingloriously. Everyone knew it.

A few days later, as David tried to slink out of Jerusalem, a man named Shimei walked on the other side of the street, cursing David and throwing stones at him. (No doubt the stones were a not-so-subtle reminder that the law of Moses ordained stoning for adultery.) Abishai, David's loyal friend, was outraged that the king should be insulted like this. "Why should this dead dog curse the king?" cried Abishai. "Let me take his head off!" "No," replied David sadly. "Shimei curses me only because God has told him to. The treatment Shimei accords me is no worse than I deserve." David was publicly humiliated, yet refused to flee his humiliation inasmuch as his public humiliation was the God-ordained consequence of his sin.

King David's greater Son did not flee his public humiliation either. Jesus was "numbered among the transgressors." He was assigned that death — crucifixion — which the Romans reserved for insurrectionists, deserters and rapists, for those whose disgrace could not be greater. He refused to flee his public humiliation inasmuch as his humiliation was the God-ordained consequence not of his sin but of his righteousness. The apostle Paul says it most compactly: "He who knew no sin was made sin for us, that in him we might become the righteousness of God."

Elijah, David, John, Jesus. The story of humankind's redemption begins with him who incarnated the flaming heart of God, as well as with those who were glad to point to him just because they too had been ignited with the same flame.

Chapter 28

FROM SOCIAL ASCENDANCY TO SALT

Salt becomes effective precisely when it seems to have come to nothing!

Gone are the glory days when the church had power and clout. Now it seems believers can only be "salt." Far from drop-in-the-bucket insignificance, salt in the "mix" of our society makes subtle yet momentous changes whose ultimate effectiveness we can safely leave in God's hands.

Toronto used to be known as "Toronto the good." In those days the buildings that towered over the city were all churches. St. James Cathedral, Anglican; St. Michael's Cathedral, Roman Catholic; Metropolitan Church, Methodist. As huge structures they rose up above everything else in the city and dominated it. Not only did church buildings dominate the city, so did church leaders. No city politician dared defy them. No public servant or board of education official would say or do anything that simply flew in the face of the church's convictions. Back in the days of Toronto the Good even a clergyman was president of the University of Toronto.

What buildings dominate Toronto's skyline now? They are all banks! Toronto Dominion was the first superstructure, followed by the Bank of Montreal, then Commerce, Royal, Nova Scotia, and Canada Trust. Clearly, it's the pursuit of money that characterizes the city. During the recession the auto manufacturers had their worst year in decades. But the banks made a profit, and the trust companies swelled. Compared to the banks the cathedral churches look like tinker-toys, the playthings of children.

There's no doubt about it. The Christian church has lost the kind of power it used to have in our society. Can you imagine a clergyman occupying the president's office at the University of Toronto today?

The fact is, we're not going to bring back the days of Toronto the Good any more than we're going to bring back the British Empire. The church is not going to have the kind of power it once had.

But this is no reason for weeping! Think of the situation in first-century Rome. The city held one million people. There were only five house churches in it. Five times 15 members equals 75 Christians in a city of one million. Yet the Christians never looked upon themselves as mere trace elements. The two New Testament books that have to do with the church in Rome are Mark's gospel and Paul's letter to the Romans. In neither book is there any suggestion of self-pity, no hint that those Christians felt themselves handcuffed or useless. They knew they were not socially ascendant. They could only be salt. They would have to be salt. So confident is Paul in the Roman Christians' saltiness (he regards 75 parts per million as a strong concentration!) that he plans to visit them only briefly before moving on into Spain where he is really needed.

We're going to have to be salt as well. Yet unlike the apostle, few today are keen on being salt. We, the church, would much rather have the kind of power we used to have. After all, we suburbanites are accustomed to power. We're achievers, goal-attainers, successful. We've obviously mastered techniques that ensure results — the technique of passing exams, of shaping metal or wood, of rising steadily on the corporate ladder. We've always predicted what it takes to reach a goal. Then we have programmed ourselves to reach the goal. We've been able to engineer the result.

Now, as individual Christians and as a church, we find we have no clout. Our society doesn't listen to our Christian convictions.

Public officials don't have to take seriously our advocacy of Christian truth. We've become a minority, a minority without the capacity to coerce.

There's only one thing we can do. We have to become salt! There is no reason for discouragement. Remember, the Christians in Rome nowhere complained they lacked clout. Instead, they had every confidence Christian salt would penetrate and permeate as salt invariably does.

As we learn what it is to have salt instead of clout we must understand something crucial: salt becomes effective precisely when it seems to have come to nothing, when it seems to have disappeared.

The effect of salt

The effect of salt is twofold: it preserves food from spoiling and brings out its richest flavour. We Christians are to be salt in both senses in our society. What we add is meant to inhibit social decomposition and to bring out, under God, human richness. But salt does this only as salt gets out of the salt shaker and into the stew. Paradoxically, once the salt is in the stew it has disappeared as salt, it would seem. But precisely when the salt has been swallowed up it becomes effective.

Yet to say we Christians lack power is not to say we lack effectiveness. We do lack the kind of power yesterday's church had in Canada. But we don't lack effectiveness. We may be only a little pinch of salt; and we may feel we've been swallowed up. Certainly we can't program results or engineer success. But this is only to say that real effectiveness can now begin.

Free to stand

Once we've decided we can only be salt many things fall into place. We are now gloriously free from concern with results and success, free to stand by our Christian convictions, free to do the truth (as John says) and keep on doing it. That capitulation you have been rationalizing for the past six weeks; a capitulation that would sabotage so much of your integrity, even leave you not knowing who you are — *resist it!* That sacrifice you were going to make just because it is the right thing to do but were hesitating over because it might not result in something big and splashy — *make it anyway!* The help you've been giving someone, help that is starting to look pointless — *go on with it!* The smallest amount of salt has some effect. Don't listen to those who say, "It's only a drop in the bucket, so why bother?" It's salt in the stew! There is a world of difference! A drop in the bucket is a quantitative change of negligible significance; salt in the stew is a qualitative change of incalculable significance.

My father taught Sunday School for dozens of years. I remember him shaking his head, one day, about Gordon Rumford, a fellow a bit older than I who misbehaved defiantly and wrote off my dad as an antiquated jerk and who eventually cavorted with a motorcycle crowd, most of which found its way to prison. "If anything comes of that fellow it will be a miracle," was my father's comment time and time again. Several years ago I was walking through a hotel lobby in Toronto when I bumped into Gordon Rumford. He told me he preached frequently at a church in Mississauga. As soon as we "bumped" he said, "It was your father. All the time I was running with the crowd that eventually went to prison I kept thinking of your father. He was so kind and patient with me even when I laughed at him. What kept me out of jail was thinking to myself, 'What would Jack Shepherd think if he could see me now?'" Salt. I asked Gordon to write my widowed mother and let her know about this. He did. More salt: his letter delighted her for weeks.

Recently I was exposed to a university professor from the U.S.A. whose professional standing is sound. He has taught well, researched thoroughly, published papers and books, and, of course, has tenure. In other words, he has it "made." He is also a Christian of Mennonite persuasion. Mennonites, everyone knows, are especially concerned with peace. This fellow has resigned his professorship and has moved himself, with his family, to Managua, Nicaragua. In Managua he will join other Mennonites in deliberate, conscientious efforts at waging peace. Is he simply silly in view of what his own government has done for decades in El Salvador and

Central America? He knows what bridges he has burnt behind him. He knows his group of Mennonites can't program any results or engineer any success. Nonetheless, the pressure of his Lord upon him constrains him to be salt; just a small pinch in a very big stew, yet a pinch whose effectiveness begins only when it seems to have come to nothing.

If today you know what stand you have to take or what step you have to take, *then take it!* When you are doing what you're convinced is right and other people are snickering at your supposed naiveness or simple-mindedness, *ignore them before you doubt yourself.* We aren't in the business of engineering results. We're in the business of a resilient, confident faithfulness whose effectiveness we can safely leave in God's hands.

The lottery setup stuns me. Lotteries have been outlawed repeatedly throughout the western world. (For 300 years in France and Great Britain.) They've been outlawed for one reason: they produce nothing but misery; social and moral wreckage. They have proven themselves, over several centuries, to be humanly ruinous. Lotteries deliberately foster an out-of-control appetite. In every era they have only degraded people. Nevertheless, when the Ontario government implemented the 6/49 set-up it cleared 90 million dollars in the last two weeks alone of the lead-up to the first draw. Obviously the lottery is going to be around for a while. The goose that lays the golden egg isn't about to be slain. (The government of Ontario will garner $100 million per year from its first casino.) Churches don't dominate Toronto's skyline anymore, just as churches don't dominate the public's mindset. Banks do. The pursuit of money does. No church group is able to pressure a politician. We can only be salt.

Salt's contribution

Our salty contribution to the stewpot is just this: by what we live for and what we can live without you and I will demonstrate that the pursuit of wealth ends in anxiety and unhappiness; the pursuit of sensuality leaves people empty and hollow; the pursuit of security only intensifies insecurity.

Nobody is going to listen to us or even notice us, it would seem. Yet precisely at this point an effectiveness will begin in the social stewpot which we may not live to see but which God has guaranteed.

If you doubt this then you should think about the Christian church in totalitarian countries. These countries have endeavoured to eradicate the Christian faith by any and all means, however vicious or cruel. The expression of church life changed dramatically. Christians in those countries had no choice but to become salt. What results could a church in the former U.S.S.R. engineer when employers, schools, government and secret police were bent on eradicating any suggestion of faith? And if you had to state, 30 or 60 years ago, which side in the struggle was more likely to emerge the winner, you would have picked the non-Christian side, in view of the enforcement it could wield. Yet there were more self-confessed Christians in the U.S.S.R. on the eve of its collapse than members of the Communist party! Salt was quietly effective for decades when it appeared to have been swallowed up and to have come to nothing. People who have no choice at being successful still have every chance to be faithful. We are never an insignificant drop in the bucket; we are salt in the stew!

Saltiness matters so much that Jesus insists that to lose our saltiness is to render ourselves a kingdom-reject. It is important that we be salt whenever, wherever, however we can. We must never abandon our own saltiness because we don't see around us leaders who support us. Instead, we must persist, for then appropriate leaders will appear in God's own time.

Our leaders reflect society

We often hear it said that any society gets the kind of leaders it deserves, since the society generates its own leaders. "If this is the case," someone says, "then our situation really is hopeless. If leaders, so-called, simply reflect the society that produces them, then we are never going to have leaders who are any better than the society that generated them. What we call 'leaders' are really nothing more than camp followers!" I certainly understand the questioner's despair. I shall make no comment on the work of the current president of the National Hockey League. For a long time, however, I stood amazed at the decisions of his predecessor, Mr. Clarence Campbell. The NHL team owners seemed to own him as well. He appeared to be their flunky. He did exactly what they wanted. He never seemed to do the right thing, the good thing, what was best for the wider society. (After all, NHL hockey *is* played in a societal context.) He never seemed to grasp the fact that the NHL player is the most adulated model for countless Canadian youngsters. And he seemed to provide pathetically little support for NHL referees who were abused by players and coaches. One day the late Stafford Symthe said proudly, "We owners wanted a league president who was intelligent, socially prominent, educated — and who would do exactly what we told him to do. And this is what we have!"

It would appear that society as a whole is no different. Our leaders appear to do exactly what their public tells them to do. Which is to say, they aren't leaders at all. They are nervous Nellies who quake in anticipation of the Gallup poll. Then there is no way of changing anything.

A new agent at work

But there is! As soon as salt, just a little salt, is added to the stewpot the salt begins to penetrate and permeate. To be sure, the stew is changed only slightly, even unnoticeably. Nevertheless, in truth there is a new factor at work. And because there is a new agent at work the slightest change is yet a profound change. The social stew is going to give rise to profoundly new leadership. Barbara Tuchman, a prominent U.S. historian, maintains that the prevailing element in American life today is false dealing. Few would care to differ with her. What would it mean, ultimately, if a few grains of salt resolved to deal differently?

Of course we often feel we are a lone voice, a lone witness. Yet insofar as we are salt the one grain that we are encourages another grain here to come forth and another grain there. It takes several grains to make a pinch. But it takes only one pinch to be effective.

Centuries ago the prophet Elijah complained that he was the only salt-grain left in Israel. "I alone have not bowed the knee to Baal," he lamented. "Don't be so presumptuous," replied God, "and stop pitying yourself. There are seven thousand in Israel who haven't bowed the knee to Baal." It takes only one person doing what he or she knows is right to encourage and call forth so many others. Many grains make one pinch. And one pinch is effective beyond our imagining.

When Jesus tells us, his disciples, that we are the salt of the earth he means exactly what he says. How effective he knows we can be is measured by his caution that our saltiness, yours and mine, we must ever retain, lest we be cast away.

Chapter 29

TO WRESTLE AND TO DANCE

There is always grace in the wilderness!

Scripture insists that God's people are always rendered able to dance. We have already tasted a deliverance fashioned through God's triumph. Yet we don't merely dance, we also struggle and fight at the same time!

"Nothing can separate us from the love of God in Christ Jesus our Lord," cried St. Paul at the climax of his weightiest theological treatise — "Nothing!" The apostle did not say this lightly. He was painfully aware of what seems to separate us from the love of God in Christ Jesus our Lord, what aims at separating us. Certainly it often leaves us feeling that we have been separated. "It" can be any one of the deadly things that afflict us, some of which Paul listed: distress, persecution, homelessness, war, hunger, relentless danger. I understand why he said these appear to drive a wedge between us and God's love. Who among us wouldn't feel (at least occasionally) separated from God's love if we were homeless, hungry or disease-ridden? Nonetheless, it is the apostle's conviction that God's love for us in Christ Jesus our Lord is so relentless and penetrating that, laser-like, it gets through to us and sustains us regardless of what is coming down on top of us. More than sustain us, it can even impel us to sing and dance and rejoice.

There is one ground for all of this, and one ground only: Jesus Christ has been raised from the dead. Because he has, his triumph can never be undone. Death could not crush him *ultimately*. The strong love of God which raised him from the dead has made you and me beneficiaries of the same strong love. This love is strong enough to get past and overturn whatever jars us, creeps up on us, or threatens to crumble us.

For this reason scripture insists that God's people are always rendered able to dance. God's people have already tasted a deliverance fashioned through God's triumph. Of course we shall dance! The psalmist says of the worshippers in the temple, "Let them praise God's name with dancing, making melody to him with timbrel and lyre." As Miriam and her women-friends looked back on their people's deliverance through the Red Sea, Miriam led her friends in dancing, exulting, "Sing to the Lord, for he has triumphed gloriously." When the Ark of the Covenant, signifying God's presence, was wrested out of the hands of the Philistines and returned to Jerusalem, David "danced before the Lord with all his might." I often imagine Israel's greatest king, outfitted in his regal splendour, cavorting in utter unselfconsciousness: he didn't know how he looked and he didn't care. After all, if you are going to dance with all your might, you *can't* care how you look! When God's people are impelled to dance, selfconsciousness gives way to new awareness of God's triumph and God's deliverance.

God fights for us

And yet God's people don't merely dance. We also struggle. We have to contend, even fight. In one of his last writings Paul said pithily, "I have fought the good fight, I have finished the race, I have kept the faith." It's plain that we "keep the faith" only as we also "fight the fight." There is a fight we have to fight if we are genuinely possessed of faith in God.

Why? Because God fights too! God fights in advance of us and fights for us. The people of Israel were on their way out of slavery in Egypt when they looked up and saw Pharaoh's forces close behind. They began to panic and shout at Moses, "Have you brought us out to die in the wilderness? We told you back in Egypt that we'd rather be slaves to the Egyptians than die in the wilderness!" Moses replied, "Fear not! See the salvation of the Lord. God will fight for us. So hold your peace."

Most people maintain they are afraid of fighting (and therefore they avoid fights). I think, however, that people are not afraid of fighting; they're afraid of losing. And not merely afraid of losing; they're afraid of being "licked"; and having been licked, they're afraid of being humiliated. What we really fear, at bottom, is devastating defeat that leaves us publicly humiliated. *This* is what we actually fear when we say we are afraid of fighting. If we knew that ultimately we couldn't be defeated at all, let alone licked, that so far from being humiliated we should one day be vindicated, then we should rise to fight as God's people are called to do.

As a matter of fact, as we shall see, God's people are called to wrestle and to dance *at the same time*. Then wrestle and dance we shall.

It's obvious that we fight properly and fight persistently only as we first dance and continue to dance. We *can* contend where we *should* contend only as we are first soaked in God's strong love and continue to be soaked in it. If we attempted to wrestle only, we should first become grim, then exhausted, and finally despairing. But if God's triumph and love surround us and seep into us, we shall keep on contending without succumbing to futility or frenzy.

No quitting

As a pastor it is my privilege to be nourished constantly by people who wrestle and dance every day. When I sat on the Board of Directors of the Peel Mental Health Housing Coalition, one of the board-members was a consumer of our services; that is, she is afflicted with schizophrenia herself. One of her worst episodes overtook her while she was worshipping in church. The police had to be called to remove her from the service. Her illness follows a pattern: she is fine for several months, and then psychotic, hallucinatory, hospitalized for four or five months, and then better again. Yet she does not hide in false shame, does not give up but rather speaks to community groups when she is well. Recently she was honoured for her community work by means of an award conferred through the Canadian Mental Health Association. She wrestles without quitting, but also without falling into "poor meism" or "why meism?" or raging resentment at those of us whose good fortune it would be so easy for her to resent.

Several years ago a man fell in love with her. He knew of her condition. There were no secrets. Yet he loved her, and they decided to marry. A psychiatrist from Mississauga Hospital carefully explained to the fellow what schizophrenia is, how severely schizophrenic people behave, how frequent the episodes are, the nature of treatment required, and so on. The man took it all in and said he loved this woman and would cherish her, illness and all. They married.

Now what we can understand with our head (understand *entirely* with our head) we cannot anticipate *at all* in our heart. And so when my friend's illness overtook her again, her husband was aghast. He *thought* he had come to terms with it; and so he had, at the level of thought. When it happened, however, it was something else. Now *he* had to wrestle — with himself, with her illness, with the commitment he had made to her. The two of them have been married for many years now, and they wrestle conjointly. Courage! Resilience! Persistence! But no whining! Their attitude to it all is, "Why should we surrender to this intruder? Why should we cower before or step around this usurper?"

Their attitude reminds me of young David (then only a teenager) in his encounter with Goliath. David came down from tending sheep in the hills only to find the men of Israel drooping. The so-called men of valour were fearful, dispirited, licked. What chance would any of them have against the seven-foot Goliath? David looked around him and said emphatically, "Who is this uncircumcised Philistine that he should defy the armies of the living God?" "Who is this self-important bully? Why do you allow this ungodly ruffian to deflect you from what God has ordained you to do?" You know the rest of the story.

Courage and persistence

As a pastor I marvel at the courage and persistence I see in people every day. The person with severe arthritis: getting up a step of eight inches is like climbing Mt. Everest. But these people do it, don't they! My physician in New Brunswick had five children and a wife who was incurably incapacitated through neurological disease. He had a large practice to maintain, five children to sort out, a wife whose condition was heartbreaking. Still he was diligent in his work, patient with people who complained petulantly of hangnails and sore throats, eager to spend 20 minutes with me (after he had diagnosed my bladder infection) telling me there weren't 25 hours in the day and the sooner I grasped this the sooner I was going to feel better. In it all he remained enthusiastically, gloriously life-affirming. "I will fight for you," said the Lord God to the people of Israel. That doesn't mean we can now do nothing; it means that our doing, our fighting, will never be in vain. And therefore we do not give up. Never. Even if the struggle is fierce.

"Beasts of Ephesus"

In his first letter to the congregation in Corinth Paul wrote, "I fought with beasts at Ephesus." The Greek word he used for "fight" means to be engaged in gladiatorial combat. But Paul was a Roman citizen, and no citizen could be forced into gladiatorial combat. Clearly he was using the word metaphorically, meaning he wrestled with opponents who were bent on dismembering the gospel. Plainly the struggle was intense; and initially, at least, he seemed to have no chance of succeeding. Yet wrestle he had to and so wrestle he did.

Make no mistake. To speak of wrestling with wild beasts is no exaggeration. A few weeks ago a 26-year-old man came to see me. He had just been released from an alcohol-treatment centre and was now working part-time (30 hours per week) for $6 per hour. He had been to prison several times for breaking-and-entering and theft. He hated prison, simply hated it, and had been badly beaten during his last imprisonment. He sat in my office and told me with transparent genuineness how fierce a struggle it is for him to stay on the street. He told me that when he gets "down" on himself and loses his confidence, resilience and hope, what bubbles up is what has been ingrained in him for years and is now second nature: theft. Minutes before he dropped in to talk with me he was walking past the church, hungry, when he looked through the front doors, saw the Foodpath baskets of food, and automatically wondered how he was going to steal it. Finally he walked around to the back door of the church and sat in the choir room until I returned from lunch. "You don't have to steal food here," I told him, "we'll give you food." I gave him what was in the Foodpath baskets. You and I have no idea how fierce the struggle is for this young man and what will surely befall him if he ever gives up the struggle. "I fought with beasts at Ephesus." Some people fight with beasts in our cities.

Few people in our churches struggle with criminality. Our areas of wrestling are different. In some cases it is an "Achilles' heel" that arose through psychological wounding incurred who knows how and when. Yet wrestle we must, for not to wrestle would be to spend the rest of our lives looking like David's countrymen who resembled whipped dogs in allowing an uncircumcised Philistine to defy the armies of the living God. Or we wrestle with a besetting temptation which has beset us for years. Capitulation would be sin; we know this, and know that our capitulation would be without excuse.

At the end of the day St. Paul says we wrestle not against flesh and blood; that is, we don't wrestle against *merely* human adversaries. All wrestling, finally, is spiritual conflict. And so it is all the more important to know that God will fight for us.

Grace in the wilderness

Yet wrestling isn't the only thing we do. We dance as well. There is celebration of little victories gained already and greater victories to come; celebration above all of him who fights for us and never forsakes us. I am moved every time I read Jeremiah's joyful exclamation at God's faithfulness and never-failing love. Listen to the prophet:

Thus says the Lord:
 "The people who survived the sword **found grace in the wilderness** . . .
 I have loved you with an everlasting love; therefore I have continued my faithfulness to you.
 Again you shall adorn yourself with timbrels, and shall go forth in the dance of the merrymakers." (Jeremiah 31:2-4)

The people who survived the sword found grace in the wilderness. To be alive, to be functioning at all, is to have survived the sword. It is certainly better than not having survived it, but it still sounds bleak. Jeremiah tells us there is also grace in whatever wilderness we happen to inhabit. We don't all inhabit the same wilderness; but we do inhabit a wilderness of some kind, even a wilderness peculiar to us. Yet it is in the wilderness that grace is promised us and grace is found.

Why is there grace in the wilderness? *How* does there come to be grace in the wilderness? The prophet again: "[Says the Lord] 'I have loved you with an everlasting love; therefore I have continued my faithfulness to you.'" The bottom line is this: "Again you shall go forth in the dance of the merrymakers."

There is one thing I want for myself above everything else. I want my demeanour, my appearance, my uncontrived face and physique to exude one message: *there is always grace in the wilderness,* and because there is, anyone at all may join in the dance of the merrymakers.   ⊕

Victor A. Shepherd, B.A., B.D., M.D., Th.D., is one of Canada's best-known scholars of the 16th century reformer John Calvin, and the 18th century theologian John Wesley. A minister of The United Church of Canada, Dr. Shepherd has served Streetsville United Church for 16 years.

In 1993 he was appointed to the chair of Wesley Studies at Ontario Theological Seminary in Toronto, where he serves as professor. He was formerly adjunct professor at The Memorial University of Newfoundland, Emmanuel College, University of Toronto, and McMaster University, Hamilton, Ontario.

For the past decade Dr. Shepherd has provided leadership to the renewal and reform movement within the United Church. He currently serves on the board of directors of Community of Concern and Church Alive and on the editorial advisory board of *Fellowship Magazine*, published by the Renewal Fellowship.

He is author of four previous books including *Making Sense of Christian Faith, Ponder and Pray*, and *So Great a Cloud of Witnesses*. He has published over 70 articles in numerous journals.

He and his wife Maureen have two daughters, Catherine and Mary.